RAILWAYS AROUN
WHITBY
VOLUME ONE

Scarborough – Whitby – Saltburn, Malton – Goathland – Whitby, Esk Valley, Forge Valley and Gilling Lines

Martin Bairstow

C000176213

A sad moment in the story of *Railways Around Whitby*. K4 2 – 6 – 0 No 3442 "The Great Marquess" pilots K1 No 62005 across Larpool Viaduct with the "Whitby Moors Railtour" on 6 March 1965. An eight coach DMU heads towards Ruswarp in the valley below.
(G W Morrison)

Published by Martin Bairstow, 53 Kirklees Drive, Farsley, Leeds
Printed by The Amadeus Press, Cleckheaton, West Yorkshire

Copyright © Martin Bairstow 2008

Introduction

The first edition of *Railways Around Whitby* appeared in 1989. It was reprinted with the tiniest amendment in 1991. It was revised in 1998, by which time it had acquired the suffix *Volume One*. This new edition is further revised, enlarged and updated.

The book begins with a tale by Stuart Carmichael who arrived at Sandsend for a week's holiday on the day the station closed. The history is then traced of the four main routes out of Whitby: to Malton, Middlesbrough, Saltburn and Scarborough. We then divert on to the Forge Valley Line, which used to link Scarborough with Pickering. The Ryedale chapter gives an outline history of the triangle of lines centred on Gilling. These are covered in much greater detail in *Railways of Ryedale*, published in 2004.

We are then drawn in to the closure period, which left Whitby with only one rail outlet. Finally we see one of the closed lines transformed into a major preserved/ heritage railway.

Railways Around Whitby Volume Two is a totally separate book, which explores a number of themes in greater depth. Published in 1996, it has been out of print for some years. Eventually, I hope to produce a new edition.

To my regret, I didn't reach Whitby until four years after the 1965 closures. My greatest regret is at the closures themselves, not just my failure get there in time. I was only 12 years old and had probably done quite well to experience as much train travel as I had. In 1964, I could easily have travelled from York to Whitby, out via Scarborough and back via Pickering. By the following year, the opportunity had gone.

Thank you to everybody who has helped with successive editions of this book. Judged by the number of copies sold, this is by far the most popular book in a series, which has so far run to 37 titles over a period of 24 years.

Contents

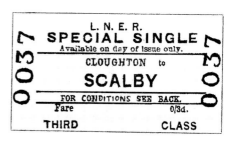

L. N. E. R.
SPECIAL SINGLE
Available on day of issue only.
CLOUGHTON to
SCALBY
FOR CONDITIONS SEE BACK.
Fare 0/3d.
THIRD CLASS
0037 0037

L. N. E. R.
CHILD
FOR CONDITIONS SEE BACK. Available for three days, including day of issue
THORNTON DALE to
SCARBOROUGH
THIRD CLASS Fare 1s 4d.C
0499 0499

One theme of this book is how to make the most of Whitby's surviving but tenuous link into the national railway network. Two Metro Cammell DMUs pass at Castleton Moor about 1966. *(D J Mitchell)*

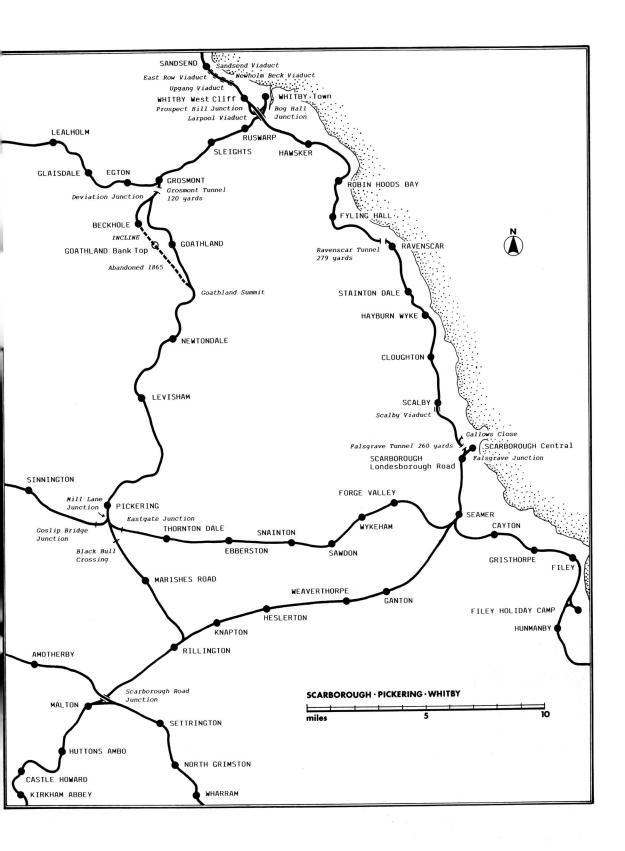

SCARBOROUGH · PICKERING · WHITBY

Camping at Sandsend
By Stuart Carmichael

The bay at Sandsend with three camping coaches at East Row and two at the Station.

(Tindales of Whitby)

In the late 1950s and early '60s most of our holidays were taken in Camping Coaches, which were ideal for a family of extended proportions as one rarely had to lug suitcases, spades and yachts more than fifty yards from the station. My father was a railwayman at that time and the privilege fares were an essential feature of the holiday budget.

I believe our first Camping Coach holiday was in 1957 at Sandsend, almost certainly in May to take advantage of the low season rates. As a ten year old I had no idea that people would do anything as pointless as spending a day at a station collecting locomotive numbers but I was sufficiently stirred by Leeds City's 'Midland Compounds' and the gleaming brass foxes on the nameplates of 'Hunts' to note their numbers in my first diary.

Little remains in my memory of that holiday except sun, sand, sea and a train ride from Sandsend to Staithes: an all-too-short fifteen minutes clinging to the cliff edge, thundering up the 1 in 57 through Sandsend Tunnel to re-appear apparently suspended in mid-air before plunging a few seconds later into Kettleness Tunnel. The pungent smell of smoke and the mellow dustiness of wooden carriages never fail to re-kindle that early excitement. It was something of an anti-climax to

have to spend four hours in Staithes at high tide until the return train.

May 1958 saw a repeat visit to Sandsend. We left the bitter cavernous gloom of Leeds City at 9.22 am behind 'Hunt' class No. 62765 'The Goathland'. If we had just been heading for Whitby, we could have changed at Malton where the 11.00 to Whitby Town was waiting in the bay platform, but that would not have enabled us to reach Sandsend. This explains why we took the longer route via Scarborough. A single change here put us on to the 11.40 direct to Sandsend.

The winter timetable offered just two through trains from Scarborough to Middlesbrough, at 11.40am and 4.24pm. There was in addition a morning train starting from Whitby Town at 7.00 for Middlesbrough and an evening one at 7.40 from Scarborough to Whitby. Normally these trains would have comprised just two coaches, which meant that they could be propelled out of Scarborough station to avoid the engine having to run round at Falsgrave Junction.

This, however, was no ordinary day. Our train was in fact the penultimate northbound working over the superbly scenic route between Whitby and Loftus. In anticipation of the occasion drawing

With brass fox nameplate, "Hunt" class D49 No 62769 "The Oakley" draws out of Scarborough Station on 31 August 1952. Falsgrave Tunnel, on the left, gives access to Gallows Close goods yard, Northstead Carriage Sidings and the line to Whitby. *(John Oxley)*

additional traffic, the load was increased to five bogies, which meant that the train had to depart from Platform 1A. This was bad news for my parents, who had to make the extra trek to the far end of Platform 1 in the hope of finding a compartment for our party of seven.

My memories of the journey behind Standard 2-6-4T No. 80116 are vague but are supplemented by a report in the August 1958 edition of *Trains Illustrated* by Mr K. Hoole, who was covering the event from the footplate.

We left Scarborough three minutes late as was normal practice when Platform 1A was in use. As soon as the engine had cleared the points leading on to the Whitby line, we changed direction and plunged into Falsgrave Tunnel. At that time the first section of line was regulated by track circuit block, so it was not until Gallows Close box that we picked up the first single-line token.

After achieving over 40 miles per hour, we were forced to slow down for the 30 mph restriction through Scalby, where the station had closed in 1953. Trains did still call occasionally to deliver customers to the four camping coaches which occupied the station yard. Further coaches were positioned along this route at Cloughton, Stainton Dale, Ravenscar, and Robin Hood's Bay.

Our first station stop was at Cloughton, where we exchanged tokens. Although on the winter timetable we were not booked to pass another train until Loftus, the greater volume of summer traffic required that this labour-intensive ritual be carried out at all the passing loops en route.

On leaving Cloughton we began to climb. Over the next five miles the gradient was to stiffen from an initial 1 in 90 to 1 in 71 on the pull out of Hayburn Wyke and finally 1 in 41, covered at just under 20mph, from Stainton Dale to the summit of

Ravenscar. As soon as we set off from Ravenscar we began to coast down the 1 in 39 overlooking the sea towards the small station at Fyling Hall. Here the porter dealt with a couple of passengers and then locked the station, which was henceforth to become unstaffed, and joined the train himself.

Leaving Robin Hood's Bay, we were again struggling to maintain 20mph on the 1½ mile climb at 1 in 43 from which one could now enjoy a view back towards Ravenscar. Once over this next summit, it was a steady drop through Hawsker and over Larpool Viaduct until we reached Prospect Hill Junction, where we joined the line out of Whitby Town for the final climb up to West Cliff Station. Here we took water and changed crews.

Once away from West Cliff it was only six minutes to Sandsend. First we descended at 1 in 60 across the viaducts at Upgang, Newholm Beck, and East Row, by which time we were virtually on the beach, then we began to climb again over Sandsend Viaduct and into the station. Here we were met by the Station Master, Mr Goodall, who later presented us with a 'last ticket' as a souvenir of what must have been a sad day for him.

We had arrived at 12.44 and a southbound train went through at 1.48. The next pair of trains would be the last. After spending part of the afternoon acclimatising ourselves to the Camping Coach, we returned to the platform where a small crowd had gathered to witness the passing of the 5.28 train for Middlesbrough.

This, the 4.24 from Scarborough, headed by class L1 2-6-4T No. 67754, was booked to pass the last southbound train at Kettleness. This was the same set upon which we had travelled, still in the care of 80116. It was two or three minutes late due to the antics of a press photographer who had nearly missed it at Kettleness.

80116 on a Scarborough to Middlesbrough "express" waits to pass a southbound train at Stainton Dale.
(N E Stead collection)

80118 disappears over Sandsend Viaduct with the 9.25am from Middlesbrough to Whitby Town on the final day of service.
(David R Smith)

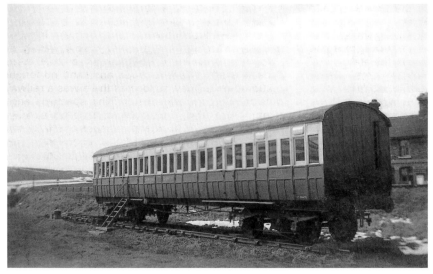

Camping Coach No 149, built 1912 for the Great Eastern Railway, at Kettleness in March 1958.
(Geoffrey Lewthwaite)

Sandsend Station and camping coaches looking south in July 1957.   *(J C W Halliday)*

As soon as the last train drew to a halt at Sandsend, carriage doors were flung open and the platform filled with running photographers. The mayhem was concluded when the same gentleman of the press, determined to get the best shot, refused the door held open for him by the Station Master and tried to board the last carriage. He misjudged the acceleration down the 1 in 62 over Sandsend Viaduct and was left behind. After that were was a feeling of emptiness, although the lack of trains in the following days did bring new opportunities.

The highlight of the previous year was being allowed to pull off a signal in the tiny Sandsend cabin, but now we were free to clamber across the track and make a direct, if precipitous, path down to the beach. Sandsend boasted two sets of green and cream Camping Coaches – a pair at the station and three at East Row which were virtually on the beach and a more attractive proposition to us lads. East Row was always booked up well in advance and we never got in there; I suspect my parents were glad as it would have meant a ¾ mile walk from the station back towards Whitby.

My overriding impressions of a Camping Coach were the sense of space and light, the heavy brass handles, leather window straps, and the smell of paraffin for lamps and cooker. We climbed along running boards, hid among bogies, fought over the top bunk and were fascinated by the window blinds. We learned from grandfather how to find rabbit runs, set a snickle, and kill and skin a rabbit. There were guinea fowl roaming alongside the track towards Hinderwell and we searched fruitlessly for their eggs.

Our morning chore was to fetch water from the station in immaculate examples of the tin-smith's craft: oval-sectioned containers with close-fitting lids and wire handles.

At the end of the week it was a disappointment to have to return to Whitby by bus, but the DMU to Scarborough was a new experience. Having lost the coastal line through Sandsend, we did at least have the compensation of the better view afforded from the new trains over the equally spectacular coastal stretches of the Scarborough and Whitby line.

The following year we stayed in a Camping Coach at Goathland, but by then I had been initiated into the rites and delights of train-spotting at Rothwell Grammar School, about a mile from Ardsley shed. The lack of sea and sand no longer mattered on holiday, as long as there was a railway outside the door, with the thrilling spectacle each afternoon of a B1, usually 61002 'Impala', rushing non-stop through Goathland in a swirl of smoke and steam on the 5.53pm to Malton and York. Our holiday this year must have been in high summer as this train only ran from the beginning of July to the end of August.

Steam was still supreme in 1959 and if there were a few DMUs they were not noted. A grimy class Q6 0-8-0 would clank through with the pick-up freight, a far cry from the highly polished T2 No. 2238 which graces the North Yorkshire Moors Railway today. One of Malton shed's pair of

The last train to call at Sandsend, the 5.44pm to Scarborough on 3 May 1958, hauled by standard 2 – 6 – 4T No 80116.
(Stuart Carmichael collection)

Standard Class 3 2-6-2T's, No. 82029, was a regular performer that summer, its determined performance up the 1 in 49 from Beckhole to Goathland signalled well in advance by its rasping exhaust and attendant plume of steam and cinders. The regulator used to remain open until it reached the start of the platform in contrast to the two 'Black Fives' and GWR 0-6-2T which shut down well before the station in the summer of 1988, when I had the pleasure of a week in one of the NYMR Camping Coaches at Goathland.

In 1959 we were woken at 6.12am by the 5.20 from Malton, but today one can enjoy a more civilised start to the day, the first train arriving from Pickering behind the Class 25 at 10.40 and awaiting the arrival of the steam-hauled train from Grosmont a couple of minutes later. I was pleased to see a different locomotive on this turn each day that I was there and I would think that only an arrival at Ingrow, on the Keighley & Worth Valley Railway could match the awesome power of a steam-powered entry to Goathland.

Our journey to Goathland was inevitably by car which was also essential for excursions. Travelling to Whitby for the day by train would have involved lengthy waits for 'connections' at Grosmont. It seems a poor strategy on the parts of BR and the NYMR to cut themselves off from the potential market in Whitby and I think the sooner that the NYMR can run through to Whitby or BR can provide real connections the better.

The current Camping Coaches at Goathland are converted from Mk. 1 stock and have better facilities in terms of cooking, washing, seating and WCs than the old coaches, but the bunks, which are laid transversely, are not as comfortable as the properly built wooden longitudinal bunks of the previous style. Heating and fire safety are vastly improved from the 1950s, when paraffin and wood panelling were the norm. Safety at Goathland has also benefitted from the installation of the footbridge, which I was pleased to see does not detract from the appearance of the station and looks as though it has always been there.

By restoring the camping coach facility, the NYMR has continued a feature of the railway scene which has almost been forgotten. The preservation of Goathland Station would have been incomplete without it.

The last campers had already gone when CC132 was seen at Goathland on 6 March 1965. – Until the NYMR brought the facility back. *(G W Allenby)*

More on Camping Coaches

From an LNER advertising leaflet, three camping coaches at the south end of Robin Hodds Bay Station.
(David Beeken collection)

Stuart Carmichael's story has prompted a deeper look into the subject of camping coaches. Assistance came in the form of advertising material in the collection of David Beeken and a feature on LNER camping coaches by C.S. Carter and A.A. MacLean in 'British Railway Journal No. 23' published in 1988.

In June 1933, the LNER hastily adapted ten old Great Northern six wheelers and placed them at the disposal of holiday makers on ten branch lines. The conversion was so crude that initially there was no gangway access between the living quarters and the sleeping compartments.

According to the first publicity, the coaches could be booked at any one of a number of listed stations on the particular line and could be moved, on request to the Station Master, to a different station on the same branch during the course of the holiday.

In 1933 there were four coaches in the Whitby area which were offered for hire as follows:

Esk Valley:
At Kildale, Castleton Moor, Danby, Lealholm or Glaisdale.

Yorkshire Coast (Scarborough-Whitby):
At Cloughton, Stainton Dale or Robin Hood's Bay.
Yorkshire Coast (Whitby-Loftus):
At Sandsend, Kettleness or Staithes.
North Yorkshire Moors:
At Goathland or Levisham.

Campers were warned that some stations such as Kettleness were remote from shops and other amenities but were advised that the Station Master, 'their best friend' would buy in provisions by prior arrangement. All linen, crockery and kitchen utensils were provided. Water and conveniences were available at the station. Access into the coach was by ladder unless it happened to be parked in a platform.

The initial scheme was a success and over the next few years the number of vehicles was increased and the standard of them improved. The LMS Railway copied the idea in 1934. By 1938 coaches were available in the Whitby area at:

Staithes	Coxwold
Kettleness (2)	Helmsley
Sandsend (2)	Kirbymoorside

East Row (3)
Robin Hood's Bay (3)
Ravenscar (2)
Staintondale (2)
Cloughton (3)
Goathland
Levisham

Forge Valley
Thornton Dale
Glaisdale (2)
Castleton Moor
Danby
Lealholm

Helmsley lost its allocation for the 1939 season. The facility to move the coach elsewhere up the branch had been withdrawn but the 1939 brochure offered the 'Touring Camping Coach' giving a week's holiday starting from York. The coach travelled by ordinary passenger train and spent three nights at Pateley Bridge, two at Aysgarth and two at Glaisdale. Alternative or longer itineraries were available by negotiation. The coach had six single sleeping compartments plus living room, kitchen and toilet and was available to individual parties of at least six people.

Camping coaches were painted in the same green and cream livery as LNER tourist stock and Sentinel railcars. It was always a condition of booking in both LNER and BR periods that the journey to the campsite was undertaken by rail.

Inevitably the Second World War put a stop to the business which was not resumed until 1952 when BR converted a number of ex Great Eastern eight wheel non corridor coaches. The number of locations was fewer. There was no deployment in Ryedale or the Upper Esk Valley whilst the Forge Valley line had been closed.

After closure of the Whitby to Loftus route in 1958, its coaches were redeployed so that the main allocation was on and around the Scarborough to Whitby line. In 1963 coaches were located as follows:

Robin Hood's Bay (5)
Ravenscar (2)
Stainton Dale (2)
Cloughton (3)

Scalby (4)
Ruswarp
Grosmont (2)
Goathland

The concentration at Robin Hood's Bay and Scalby may have been due to the availability of electricity. Elsewhere bottled gas was used for lighting, heating and cooking.

Scalby Station had closed to regular passenger traffic on 28 February 1953 after which part of the station building was made available as a camping cottage. Trains continued to stop on summer

An LNER publicity photo, taken at Cloughton in 1934. No 42082 was a Great Northern six wheeler of 1885 vintage.   *(Andrew McRae collection)*

Another publicity photograph showing campers entering into the spirit of things at Forge Valley, where a coach was stationed each year up to 1939.   *(Andrew McRae collection)*

Saturdays for the convenience of camping coach and cottage patrons. Hayburn Wyke Station was also used as a camping cottage.

1964 was the last season during which camping facilities were available on the North Eastern Region of British Railways. The only four coaches outside the Whitby area were at Bolton Abbey, Newbiggin on Sea and two at Hornsea. By the spring of 1965, these stations had suffered the same fate as those on the Scarborough-Whitby and Malton-Whitby lines. Camping coaches lingered on for a few more years on other BR regions.

The Preservation Era

Even if routes such as Scarborough to Whitby had remained open, it is unlikely that camping coaches could have lasted. Stations would have lost the staff, upon whom the operation depended. They would even have lost their toilets. Meanwhile, public expectations would have risen beyond the basic facilities of the camping coach.

At first glance, it is surprising that the concept has not found much favour with preserved railways. Actually, it has for volunteer/ staff accommodation but not for commercial letting. Possibly, the

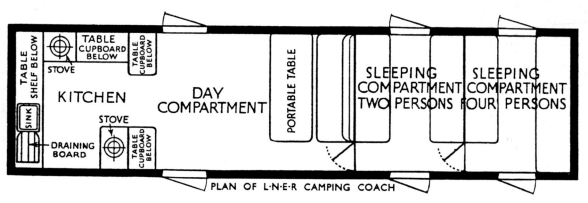

PLAN OF L·N·E·R CAMPING COACH

responsibilities are too great on lines with all volunteer staff and limited operational hours.

The exception is the North Yorkshire Moors Railway, which now offers accommodation in coaches at Goathland and Levisham and in the Station House at Grosmont. All three are available on a year round basis, though the prices are seasonal. Standards are more than a little higher than the traditional camping coach. The only concessions to tradition are the livery, fleet numbers and location of the two coaches.

The coaches mentioned in Stuart's feature were those at Goathland during the 1970s and 80s. 59098 and 59099 were trailer first/ buffet cars from Glasgow to Edinburgh DMUs, built 1960 and withdrawn in 1972. They were scrapped in 1994, having not been used in their last few years.

The present Goathland coach was built in 1951 to a Great Western design. It was converted for use as a camping coach at Ilderton in Northumberland,

attached to a restaurant in the former station. The business failed. The building became a residence but the coach was purchased by the NYMR. It is numbered CC172 in the camping coach sequence. It reopened the NYMR camping coach enterprise in 1999.

The Levisham coach has been on site since 2004. It is a BR mark 1 corridor brake, No 35270, now CC176. The intervening three numbers had been allocated to staff accommodation vehicles, CC173 and 174 at Goathland and 175 at Pickering.

The third facility offered by the NYMR is the Station House at Grosmont, which dates from the conversion from horse to steam power in 1847. It was fully refurbished for use as holiday accommodation in 2006.

On closed lines, an ex BR mark 1 is available as a camping coach at Cloughton, whilst three mark 2s are offered as holiday accommodation at Ebberston.

Camping Coach No 172 at Goathland in 2006.   (Martin Bairstow)

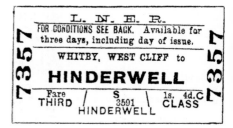

The Whitby & Pickering Railway

The story of Railways Around Whitby predates the main thrust of railway expansion by a good twelve years. When the Act for the Whitby & Pickering Railway was passed in May 1833, it was for a purely local venture which stopped short of making full use of technology which was available even then. It was to be a low cost line for horse power only with probably no thought of it ever becoming part of a national system of railways.

At that stage the only existing railway in Yorkshire was the Stockton & Darlington which had been extended to Middlesborough in 1830. The idea of a railway connecting Whitby with the Stockton & Darlington was rejected by George Stephenson on the grounds that it would not be able to compete with coastal shipping. The function of railways was to put the interior of the country in communication with the ports.

Stephenson favoured the Whitby & Pickering project which was to cut through the very difficult terrain between the coast and the Vale of Pickering. If goods could be conveyed that far by rail, then onward transport by road was just about practicable.

It was whilst working on the project, that Stephenson the engineer made the acquaintance of George Hudson the entrepreneur who happened to be visiting some inherited property in the district. The association which followed this chance meeting was to play a major part in determining the shape of the future rail network. It also ensured that George Stephenson would not in future need to be bothered with enterprises as small as the Whitby & Pickering Railway.

The main engineering features of the railway were the nine crossings of the River Esk between Whitby and Grosmont all on wooden bridges, the castellated tunnel at Grosmont and the rope worked incline between Beck Hole and Goathland, 1500 yards in length at a maximum gradient of 1 in 10.

'Motive power' was achieved on the self balancing principle. The descending train was always heavier than the ascending one by virtue of a water tank which could be filled from a reservoir at the top and then emptied into a stream at Beck Hole before being dragged back up to the top by a team of horses.

A trial run was made between Whitby and Grosmont on 15 May 1835 using a carriage called 'Premier'. This was basically a stage coach on flanged wheels. Six passengers could sit inside, four outside at the front, another four at the back and a few on top. The driver sat on top and a guard seems also to have been employed. A public service operated over this first six and a quarter miles of the railway from 8 June 1835.

The railway was completed throughout in time for formal opening on 26 May 1836 although there may have been some traffic carried to Pickering prior to that day. An account of the celebrations was written by Thomas Clark, Esq., the Treasurer of the Railway and published in 'The Scenery of the Whitby & Pickering Railway' by Henry Belcher. Crowds assembled outside the Angel Inn, Whitby, in good time for the procession to the station which began at 7.30am to the accompaniment of the Whitby Brass Band.

There appear to have been at least six carriages available to guests and these were drawn individually by horses. At Grosmont the party paused to admire the lime kilns under construction – a development which was attributed to the advent of the railway. Another promising source of traffic was the Whitby Stone Company beyond Grosmont and the guests were treated to a demonstration of a wagon loaded with stone being lowered down an incline from the hillside quarry. At Beck Hole the horses were detached and the passenger vehicles, which had been coupled together, were hauled up the incline at 'a pleasing, rapid and easy pace'.

A fresh set of horses then took over for the next

A8 class 4 – 6 – 2T at Whitby Town in the mid 1950s. The tall signal box was necessary to give a view over the goods shed.
(D Ibbotson collection)

stage to the summit of the line. In normal working the horses might then have earned themselves a ride in a dandy cart attached to the train before resuming their task at the point about four miles short of Pickering where the gradient became insufficient to proceed any further by gravity. On the opening day the horses were left behind at the Summit and the carriages, coupled together, were allowed to reach a speed of 30mph on the downgrade if Mr Clark's report is to be believed. A fresh team of horses completed the last leg of the journey into Pickering where a band was waiting to escort the party to the Black Swan. Here they 'sat down to a most excellent déjeuner à la fourchette'.

Highlight of the return journey occurred during the descent of the incline when passengers were given a demonstration of the precision with which the guard could stop the train 'in the midst of its rapid downward course'. Arrival back in Whitby was at 5pm. Guests then returned to the Angel Inn where the celebration went on until two the following morning.

The railway then settled down to an every day existence. There were normally two passenger services each way daily except Sundays. 'Bradshaw' for 1844 shows the principal departure from Whitby at 8am. This took about 2½ hours to Pickering whence a stage coach went on to York there to connect with main line trains which had been able to reach that City from London and the Midlands since 1840. A second 'luggage train' at lower fares left Whitby at 2pm and was advertised to reach Pickering at six. In the other direction the 'luggage train' left Pickering at noon. Passengers on the 'express' service left York at midday in order to catch the 3.30pm from Pickering which brought them into Whitby at six.

Compared to what had been possible before the railway, the above arrangements were revolutionary but by the mid 1840s the pace of the Whitby & Pickering Railway was rapidly being overtaken by developments elsewhere. Horse operation was not only slow but very labour intensive. A horse could only pull one vehicle and it was necessary to 'double head' on the long up grade

G5 No 67330 and A8 Nos 69864 and 69865 outside Whitby Shed on 3 September 1952. Whitby loco shed was built in 1868 to replace the Y&NM structure dating from 1847. It closed in April 1959 but remains standing. The North Yorkshire Moors Railway missed a chance to buy it. *(John Oxley)*

2 – 6 – 4T No 80116 shunting fish vans at Whitby Town about 1956. Five of these locos, 80116 - 20 were delivered new to Whitby from Brighton Works in 1955. They were all transferred away before the shed closed in 1959. *(J Davenport)*

1095

BRITISH RAILWAYS (N) (Series 17)
PLATFORM TICKET 1d.
This ticket is issued subject to the Bye-laws, Regulations and Conditions contained in the Publications & Notices of & applicable to the Railway Executive
Available ONE HOUR on DAY of ISSUE ONLY NOT VALID IN TRAINS. Not Transferable
WHITBY
To be given up when leaving Platform.

1095

Viewed from the top of Larpool Viaduct, a Middlesbrough bound DMU passes Whitby gas works in 1966. Weeds are beginning to take over the Scarborough line which, at that time, was possibly going to reopen as far as a potash mine near Hawsker.

(D J Mitchell)

A Goathland to Whitby DMU at Ruswarp in early 1965. Only the right hand platform remains. The level crossing is controlled by flashing lights. The signal box has gone but the main building survives in private ownership.

(D J Mitchell)

Sleights looking west in September 1972.

(Alan Young)

Deviation Junction box marked the divergence between the 1865 "main line" and the branch to Beck Hole. This is now the site of the NYMR loco sheds.

(G W Allenby)

The Beckhole branch saw a passenger service, summer only, between 1908 and 1914. An "autocar" is seen at the terminus.

(Martin Bairstow collection)

Class J25 No 65671 surmounts the 1 in 49 climb up to Goathland Station with a freight on 1 August 1951.

(D Butterfield)

The York & North Midland Railway

This Hudson enterprise, as its name suggests, was formed to link York with the North Midland Railway at Altofts Junction just north of Normanton. Its completion on 1 July 1840 placed York at the end of a continuous railway from London and the Midlands. The York & North Midland Railway became a part of the North Eastern Railway in 1854. By that time it had extended to Scarborough, which George Hudson predicted would be turned into the 'Brighton of the North' and it had also ended the isolation of the Whitby & Pickering Railway. Hudson also had plans to develop the town of Whitby. In 1847 he started the Whitby Building Company which acquired some fields at West Cliff and started to cover the area with streets and terraced houses. Hudson's downfall in 1848 ended his personal involvement in the development of Whitby which was probably retarded as a result.

The railway from York to Scarborough with its branch to Pickering was authorised on 4 July 1844 and opened within the incredible space of one year and three days. This feat would not have been possible if the company had opted for a tunnel through the Howardian Hills but it chose instead to let the line meander with the River Derwent for nearly four miles. It is this which provides the York to Scarborough line with its main scenic attraction albeit at the cost of a long 45mph restriction.

A week before the arrival of its first train in Pickering, the York & North Midland Railway obtained Parliament sanction to take over the Whitby & Pickering Railway which it proceeded to purchase for about three quarters of what it had cost to build. Over the next two years, the horse worked line was rebuilt with double track of heavier construction to take steam locomotives. Bridges were rebuilt in iron, a new tunnel was bored at Grosmont, some of the worst curves were eased and the hemp rope used to operate the incline was replaced by a steel one driven by steam power.

Steam operation began throughout to Whitby in July 1847. A loco shed was built at Beck Hole to house the engines at the northern end of the line which, once they had been lowered down the incline, tended to stay semi permanently to work that section.

The incline was an impediment which the North Eastern Railway took steps to overcome in its Act of 11 July 1861. This authorised a deviation line running for 4½ miles from a point south of Grosmont Tunnel to rejoin the earlier route just short of Goathland Summit. The new route opened on 1 July 1865. Built mostly on a 1 in 49 climb, it included a new station at Goathland. The old line was abandoned apart from the retention of a single track between Deviation Junction and Beck Hole. This was used to carry freight, mainly coal, to the isolated community at Beck Hole right until 1951 when a road was built. In 1908 a Summer only

Grosmont Station in July 1957, looking towards the Tunnel, through which Deviation Junction Box is just visible. *(J C W Halliday)*

A scene which anticipates the preservation era. K4 No 3442 "Great Marquess" at Goathland with a filming special on 13 April 1964. *(D J Mitchell)*

The same train leaving Goathland on its return journey from Whitby to York. *(D J Mitchell)*

passenger service was re-introduced between Whitby and Beck Hole but it ceased on the outbreak of the First World War.

A curve east of Rillington off the Whitby line towards Scarborough was opened on the same day as the deviation to permit through working between the two coastal resorts albeit by a fairly circuitous route.

The 1½ hour journey evidently failed to generate sufficient traffic so the curve only lasted for just over a year. It was then removed even though some years were still to elapse before construction of any more direct route between Whitby and Scarborough.

'Bradshaw' for April 1910 shows a winter service of six trains each way over the Whitby & Pickering line. Departures from Whitby Town were at 7.22, 8.35 and 9.15am and at 12.10, 3.50 and 7.00pm. All ran to Malton where connections to York were generally quite reasonably. Some trains were shown as only stopping by request at Marishes Road. On a Sunday there was just one train at 6.00pm which was in fact the only advertised train from Whitby by any route on the seventh day. The corresponding inward working was at 6.10 in the morning from Malton.

The basic year round service never differed greatly from the pattern described above. At closure in March 1965 there were five trains each way plus two workings between Whitby and Goathland. There was no service on Winter Sundays. It was during the summer months that the line carried additional scheduled trains and excursions. Traffic built up in the 1930s as holidays and day trips to the coast became affordable by more people.

The missing track

The track between New Bridge and Levisham was singled during the First World War to free materials for other use. This could have meant laying sidings at munitions works, or similar use in this country. It doesn't necessarily mean that the track would have been sent to the Western Front.

The second track was never reinstated, despite the receipt of compensation from the Government. Why not has been the subject of research by Graham Reussner and David R Smith, published in *Moors Line* (Summer 1996 and Spring 1999).

During 1916, the Railway Executive Committee, which exercised wartime Government control, asked the railway companies to release little used sidings and even sections of running line where double track could, temporarily be reduced to single.

On Sunday 31 December 1916, a full engineering possession was taken between New Bridge and Levisham. Points and interlocking were disconnected and electric tablet instruments installed. By late afternoon, single line working had been installed over the former down (northbound) track. The intermediate box at Farworth was a casualty of the singling.

A similar thing happened between Speeton and Bempton on the Scarborough to Bridlington line and between Enthorpe and Southburn on the line from Market Weighton to Driffield. In both these cases, double track was restored about 1924.

Redoubling between New Bridge and Levisham seems to have been intended about the same time

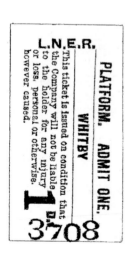

A three car Metro Cammell DMU with parcels van in tow crosses on to the single line as it pulls away from Levisham, bound for York in 1964.
(John Birkbeck)

but never carried out. Two possible explanations were unearthed, both of which may be valid. Graham Reussner discovered a suggestion that not all the materials recovered by singling were handed to the Government. Some were used for renewals elsewhere on the NER. Faced with having to pay about a quarter of the cost itself, the LNER decided that it could manage with single track.

David R Smith delved deeper into LNER records and came up with an answer, which does not rule out the previous explanation. During 1925, the Government presented the LNER with a number of counter claims, arising from the settlement in 1921 when wartime control ended. Some of these had nothing whatever to do with track reinstatement. The scale of the claims was such that the LNER had to cut back on planned expenditure. There being "no immediate necessity" to redouble New Bridge to Levisham, the work was postponed indefinitely.

The line between Rillington and Mill Lane Junction, Pickering, was never physically singled but, from the 1940s until closure, it was capable of being worked on the down track only to release the up line for wagon storage.

Richard Pulleyn remembers the staff and ticket equipment at Mill Lane and the king lever which changed the method of working but he can only recall double line block actually being in use. The summer 1964 timetable shows no ordinary passenger trains booked to pass on the section though there was one moment in the day when it would have been very tight at Rillington if the 4.08pm from Malton had been forced to wait the 4.04pm from Pickering coming off the branch.

There was a facing cross over at Mill Lane, installed in 1924 to allow access onto the Gilling line when Goslip Bridge Junction was abolished. Malton bound trains could thus cross over onto the down line and then go back via the trailing cross over at Rillington. For the final 16 months to July 1966, when Pickering was open for freight, the "branch" from Rillington was worked with a "one engine in steam" staff on the down track only.

A Metro Cammell twin set drifts into Goathland with a Whitby service in February 1965. *(Charles Allenby)*

Goathland Summit was a block post in BR days. It was at one stage planned that the North Yorkshire Moors Railway would build a terminus here.
(D Ibbotson collection)

The remoteness of Levisham Station, looking north in 1965.
(D J Mitchell)

The driver of a York to Whitby DMU accepts the single line token for Levisham at New Bridge box in the Summer of 1964.   *(John Birkbeck)*

Pickering looking north about 1949. The overall roof was removed in 1952. The North Yorkshire Moors Railway has ambitions to reinstate it.
(Martin Bairstow collection)

Six Pickering signal boxes. From top left: New Bridge *(D Ibbotson)*, High Mill, Bridge Street, Hungate and Mill Lane Junction *(John Bateman)* and Eastgate Crossing on the Forge Valley Line. *(Martin Bairstow)*

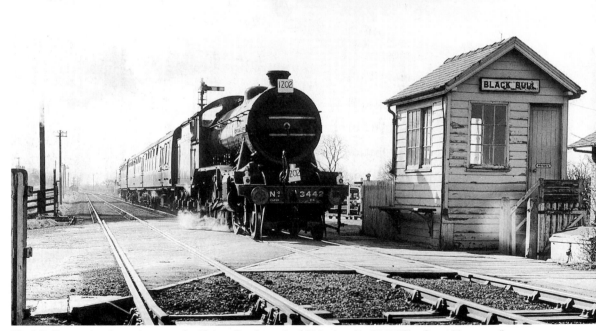

Black Bull was a level crossing over the Malton Road, south of Pickering. No 3442 "The Great Marquess" heads towards Whitby with its three coach special on 13 April 1964. *(G W Morrison)*

The 8.55am Whitby to Malton remained steam hauled because it was the return working of the early morning mail and parcels train. B1 No 61049 enters Pickering on 13 April 1964.   *(D J Mitchell)*

80116 passing Marishes Road with the 11am Malton to Whitby on 7 August 1957.   *(M Mitchell)*

Malton looking east in August 1965. The following year, the outer platform was removed so that York bound trains must cross over to use the one remaining platform. The signalling was also rationalised with the West and Station boxes closing in favour of a switch panel in the East box. (John Bateman)

Inside the train shed, facing Scarborough in 1956. The retractable bridge gave access to the outer platform. (H C Casserley)

L.N.E.R.
PLATFORM. ADMIT ONE.
(Series 3)
MALTON
1
THE HOLDER IS PROHIBITED FROM ENTERING THE COMPANY'S TRAINS.
NOT TRANSFERABLE
FOR CONDITIONS SEE BACK
D.
5258

A Derby built DMU, later class 108, in the Whitby bay at Malton. In 1989, the overall roof was removed and part of the Whitby bay canopy was re sited to provide shelter over the one surviving platform. (John Birkbeck)

North of Whitby

The Stockton & Darlington Railway

Railways came early to Teesside. The Stockton & Darlington, the world's first public railway, was opened on 27 September 1825. It was extended along the Tees to Middlesbrough in 1830, Redcar in 1846 and to Saltburn in 1861.

The present diesel service which runs hourly from Bishop Auckland and half hourly from Darlington through Middlesbrough to Saltburn uses the original Stockton & Darlington line for part of the journey. At the time of its amalgamation with the North Eastern in 1863, the Stockton & Darlington extended into Weardale and across the Pennines to Tebay on the West Coast Main Line. Its territory also included the line to Guisborough which provided the first link in establishing a railway from Middlesbrough towards Whitby.

The Middlesbrough & Guisborough Railway

The Pease family had been instrumental in establishing the Stockton & Darlington Railway and the port of Middlesbrough. In the early 1850s they purchased the rights to mine ironstone at Cod Hill, near Guisborough. They then persuaded the Stockton & Darlington to lend its support in the promotion of the Middlesbrough & Guisborough Railway. This was authorised by an Act of June 1852 but there was difficulty raising the required share capital until Messrs Pease stepped in with an offer to guarantee the dividend.

The ten mile line opened for goods traffic on 11 November 1853. It was double track and included the climb at 1 in 44 for 1½ miles between Ormesby and Nunthorpe. A passenger service was introduced in February 1854.

The mine at Cod Hill was served by a branch which climbed at 1 in 54 from Low Cross Junction, east of Pinchinthorpe, for a distance of just under a mile.

Then trains had to be drawn up a rope worked incline to reach the mine itself. The branch was short lived closing about 1865 but this apparent setback did not prevent the development of traffic from numerous other mines which opened in the Guisborough area between 1850 and 1880.

The Guisborough line was worked by the Stockton & Darlington which found itself in the enviable position of serving both the ironworks of Country Durham and the sources of the iron ore in Cleveland. It was a logical step for the S & D to consolidate its position by absorbing the Middlesbrough & Guisborough Railway in 1858 on terms which guaranteed the M & G shareholders a dividend of 6% per annum. Many small railways were forced to sell out to their larger neighbours on far less favourable terms. Such was the importance of the iron ore traffic which soon tempted an alternative railway to try and break the S & D monopoly.

The Cleveland Railway

This was a rival line running more or less parallel with the Middlesbrough & Guisborough then continuing towards Loftus. It was backed by the West Hartlepool Harbour & Railway Company which hoped to gain a stake in the lucrative iron ore traffic south of the Tees by means of a ferry to carry wagons across the river to link up with its own system near Port Clarence.

Despite strenuous opposition from the Stockton & Darlington, the Cleveland Railway was incorporated by an Act of July 1858 but was authorised only to build the section east of Guisborough. The House of Commons Committee advised the promoters to link up at Guisborough with the Stockton & Darlington whom the Committee felt sure would afford every possible accommodation for Cleveland traffic otherwise it would be open to the Cleveland Railway to make a fresh application for an independent line.

The present Middlesbrough Station was opened on 3 December 1877. The overall roof was destroyed by German bombing in August 1942. The view is from the south west.
(Martin Bairstow collection)

Not content, the Cleveland came before Parliament the following year with a new bill claiming that circumstances had changed and that they needed to get direct to the Tees at Normanby in order to load ships with iron ore for export. The new Bill was passed by the Commons but defeated in the Lords. Their Lordships did however offer the advice that a private line might be built without an Act to take ironstone from the Eston area to the Tees.

Under the title of the Upsall, Normanby & Ormesby Railway, such a private line was staked out down to a pier on the Tees at Normanby. In August 1860 the Tees Conservancy Commissioners, who appeared to share the Stockton & Darlington's distaste for the new intruder sought an injunction on the grounds that the pier would be a hazard to shipping. The court failed to agree whereupon the Conservancy adopted an alternative method of opposition.

On 10 September the Conservancy hired an army of barges which it positioned so as to prevent work on the pier but the Cleveland Railway recruited its own hands to break the moorings and send the barges away. The space intended for the pier was then enclosed by chains attached to large buoys and the same fleet of barges was bought off to come and protect the Cleveland works. During the night the Conservancy 'forces' sailed down the river in three steam tugs intending to damage the works which they expected to be unprotected. Hardly had they got started than they were attacked by the same barges who had been on their side in the morning.

After some fighting, the three tugs were driven away in a shower of stones, slag and lumps of iron.

In November 1860, the owner of Guisborough Estate, who was also one of the promoters of the Cleveland Railway, began work on a private line across his land supposedly to carry his own traffic onto the Upsall, Normanby & Ormesby Railway. In truth his purpose was to complete the link to the Cleveland Railway at Guisborough. The Stockton & Darlington asked the court to prevent a bridge being built over their line outside Guisborough Station but without success.

It only remained for the Cleveland Railway to apply to Parliament to turn these bits of partly constructed private railway into a public concern. Still under protest from the Stockton & Darlington and the Tees Conservancy, Parliament decided that it was in the public interest to end the uncertainty so, under the Cleveland Railway Act 1861, the company was empowered to complete the railway from Normanby Jetty, on the Tees, right through to Loftus.

Because work was well advanced before the line had become 'public', it took only until 23rd November 1861 to open the section from Normanby Jetty to Skelton near Guisborough. It crossed over the Stockton & Darlington near Cargo Fleet and also outside Guisborough but at neither point did it make any physical connection initially.

The Cleveland Railway was extended to Boosbeck in 1862, and to Brotton in 1865. Skinningrove was reached in 1866 but the final link

Despite loss of the overall roof, the main building survives and was cleaned up during the 1980s. The view is from the south east. *(Martin Bairstow)*

A8 No 69860 ready to leave Middlesbrough for Whitby in April 1958. The van traffic includes luggage in advance and live chickens.

(J C W Halliday)

The 140 lever box at Guisborough Junction.

(John Bateman)

A8 No 69862 calls at Ormesby with a southbound train from Middlesbrough. The 45 locos of class A8 were rebuilt after 1931 out of the H1 4 – 4 – 4Ts dating from 1913. They were all withdrawn in 1957 –60.

(N E Stead collection)

A Metro Cammell (class 101) DMU pauses at Nunthorpe on its way to Whitby on 21 August 1988. There is a lot of new housing at Nunthorpe which, since December 2007, has seen an increase in its service to Middlesbrough.

(Martin Bairstow)

Hutton Junction in April 1958. Straight ahead, the line to Loftus climbing to join the original Cleveland Railway. To the left, the Guisborough branch. In 1932, Guisborough Station box was closed and Hutton Junction box renamed Guisborough. The branch was then worked as two single lines, one for goods and one for passengers.

(J C W Halliday)

Class O (later G5) No 1319 at Eston. The short branch off the truncated Cleveland Railway was authorised by the NER Act of 1895 and opened on 1 January 1902. Eston closed to passengers and parcels on 9 March 1929 but retained a coal depot until October 1966.

(Martin Bairstow collection)

2 – 6 – 4T No 80118 at the buffer stop end of Guisborough Station.   *(E E Smith)*

A Q6 class 0 – 8 – 0 crossing Upleatham Viaduct, between Saltburn and Brotton with a mixed freight in May 1955.   *(J Davenport)*

Hutton Gate was a private station for the Pease family. It became a public station on 1 January 1904. It was an unstaffed halt from 11 September 1961 until closure on 29 February 1964 It is now a private house.

(Alan Young)

A WD 2 – 8 – 0 passing through Brotton on freight.
(T E Rounthwaite)

Skinningrove, looking south, closed as a public station in 1952 but remained as an unadvertised workmens halt until 1958. The track on the left is the start of the zig-zag.

(Alan Young collection)

into Loftus had to await completion of Kilton Viaduct. This consisted of iron girders supported by twelve stone piers which carried the railway at a maximum height of 150 feet above the Kilton Beck.

In order to reach the mines and gasworks in the valley below Skinningrove, a zig-zag line was built. The first leg started north of Skinningrove Station and ran for almost ¾ mile falling at up to 1 in 37 before ending in a reversing neck underneath Kilton Viaduct.

The second leg was much steeper at 1 in 28. This ended in another reversing neck from which trains could proceed along the valley floor to the various sidings. Trains were generally worked with an engine at each end or sometimes with two banking engines at the rear which led the train up the middle leg of the zig zag. They would uncouple from the train prior to banking up the final leg so that they could drop off as soon as the train was under way on the main line.

In 1865, the North Eastern Railway further consolidated its local monopoly by taking over the West Hartlepool Company and with it the Cleveland Railway. It immediately took steps to eliminate the duplication of routes by closing a section of the Cleveland Railway between Guisborough and Flatts Lane. First it built a short connection linking the Cleveland to the former Middlesbrough and Guisborough line at Hutton Junction. This created a through route from Middlesbrough to Loftus but with Guisborough station at the end of a short branch.

The remaining bit of the Cleveland north of Flatts Lane was connected in February 1865 to the Middlesbrough – Redcar line and continued to serve as a goods branch for just over 100 years until October 1966. From 1902 until 1929 a passenger service operated along this line from Middlesbrough to Eston which was reached by a short spur curving off at Flatts Lane.

The foundations of Kilton Viaduct were undermined by ironstone workings and in 1911 traffic had to be suspended for two years. During this period passengers were conveyed by a char-a-banc between Skinningrove and Loftus but freight, including iron-stone from Liverton Mines, had to be conveyed to Middlesbrough via Whitby and the Esk Valley line. The viaduct was buried by tipping spoil from various local mines so as to create an embankment across which rail traffic resumed in 1913. The reversing neck of the Skinningrove zig-zag line had to be realigned because previously it had run underneath the viaduct.

The Saltburn Extension

The 1865 Act which merged the Cleveland Railway into the NER also authorised the connecting line between Saltburn and Brotton.

This opened for goods on 1 July 1872 allowing traffic from the mines in the Brotton and Loftus areas to travel direct to the various works on the Tees east of Middlesbrough.

On 1 April 1875, a passenger service was introduced between Saltburn and Loftus serving Brotton and Skinningrove Stations. North Skelton

Loftus was in similar style to Brotton. 2 – 6 – 4T No 80118 calls with a southbound train.   *(R J Buckley)*

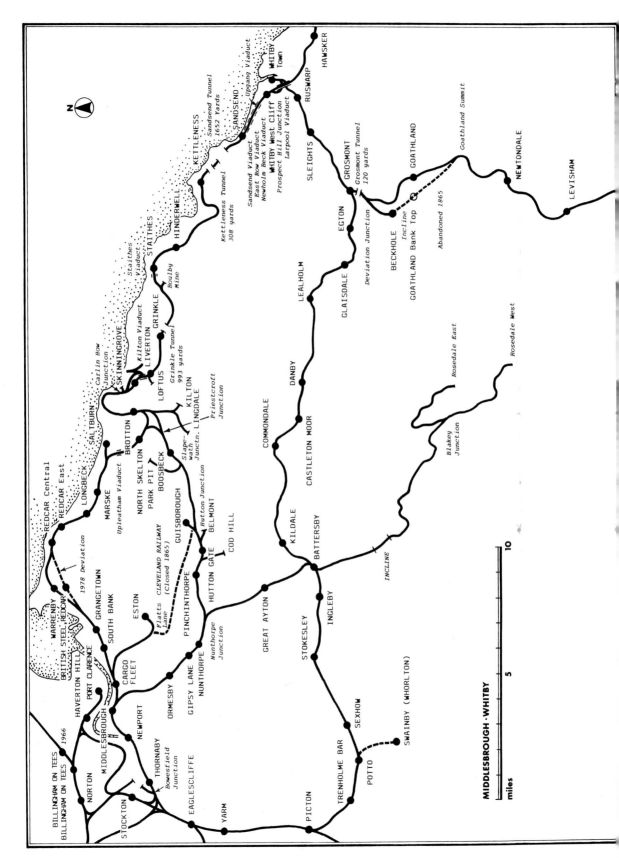

MIDDLESBROUGH-WHITBY

miles

GUISBOROUGH formerly Hutton Junction

STATION

GOODS YARD

PASSENGER BRANCH

GOODS BRANCH

LOCO SHED

SPRING

STATION GF
No. 20 Release

TO BROTTON

3/3AT

DOWN MAIN

UP MAIN

TO MIDDLESBROUGH

26 Lever CD Frame
Spare: 21
22/26 Mechanically worked colour-lights.

SKETCH FROM SB DIAGRAM AS AT 1964

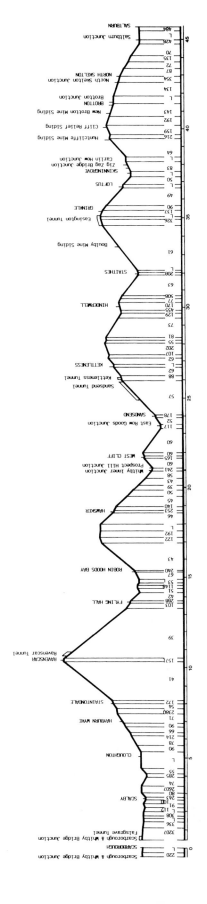

33

did not open until 1902. Trains leaving Saltburn had to propel back to the junction before joining the extension line which climbs in a long sweep encircling the town.

Also authorised under the 1865 Act was the Priestcroft Curve between North Skelton and Boosbeck. This opened in 1878 permitting a passenger service to operate from Saltburn to Guisborough. Trains had to reverse into and out of both termini and, in the twentieth century, the service became an obvious candidate for push-pull operation. Most trains also reversed at Brotton and after the First World War there were no regular passenger workings over the Priestcroft Curve.

In 1910 departures for Middlesbrough (weekdays only) for the Guisborough line were at:

6.20am to	Loftus
8.40	Loftus
9.42	Saltburn via Priestcroft Loop
11.57	Saltburn via Priestcroft Loop
12.51pm	Guisborough
2.47	Saltburn via Brotton
4.52	Saltburn via Brotton
5.17	Guisborough
6.00	Guisborough
8.20	Guisborough with connection to Saltburn via Brotton
10.48	Guisborough (Wed and Sat only)

The Whitby, Redcar & Middlesbrough Union Railway

The long business of completing the coastal railway between Whitby and Loftus began in July 1866 with the incorporation of the Whitby, Redcar & Middlesbrough Union Railway. Finance for the project was not readily forthcoming and it was not possible to start construction until 1871. Work stopped in 1874 when the contractor went into liquidation. This event was not entirely unforeseen by the railway company which had taken a charge over two of the contractor's locomotives and which it proceeded to sell.

The next task was to find an alternative way of completing the railway and for this the company turned to the NER which took a perpetual lease over the WR & MU in July 1875. The NER employed a contractor of rather more substance who found his predecessor's work, such as it was, to have been unsatisfactory. In particular it was necessary to abandon part of the cliff edge route north of Sandsend because it had collapsed into the sea during the period when work was suspended. Instead Sandsend and Kettleness Tunnels, respectively 1,652 and 308 yards in length, were driven to take the railway through the headlands rather than go round them.

It took until 3rd December 1883 before the 16½ mile route was ready for use.

In addition to the splendid coastal scenery, the railway from Whitby to Loftus was distinguished by the five steel tubular viaducts the principal dimensions of which were:

	Length	Height	Spans
Upgang	330ft	70ft	6
Newholm Bank	330ft	50ft	11
East Row	528ft	30ft	8
Sandsend	268ft	63ft	8
Staithes	790ft	152ft	17

The first four were all located within the space of 1½ miles. Staithes was by far the longest, highest and the most exposed. Traffic over it was protected by a wind gauge which rang a bell in Staithes signal box when the wind pressure reached 28lbs per square foot. At that point traffic had to be suspended. If a train was already on its way from Grinkle, it would be stopped at the Staithes outer home signal and if necessary propelled back to Grinkle. The Station Master at Staithes had to send for the nearest platelayer to make an examination of the viaduct.

No 1080 lifting a Scarborough train away from Saltburn Junction about 1902.

(LCGB Ken Nunn collection)

H1 class 4 – 4 – 4T No 1330 emerging from the north end of the 993 yard Grinkle Tunnel about 1932. The loco, dating from 1921, was rebuilt in 1934 as an A8 class 4 – 6 – 2T. It survived as BR No 69889 until 1960.   *(D Ibbotson)*

An Ivatt 2 – 6 – 0 heading north over Staithes Viaduct on 13 July 1957.   *(J C W Halliday)*

Camping Coach No 130 at Staithes on 22 March 1958.
(Geoffrey Lewthwaite)

Hinderwell for Runswick Bay, seen from a northbound train on 26 April 1958.
(J C W Halliday)

Kettleness looking south on 22 March 1958, with a wagon on the coal drop.
(Geoffrey Lewthwaite)

H1 class No 1327 emerging from the 308 yard Kettleness Tunnel with a northbound working in the early
1930s.   *(D Ibbotson)*

The same type of engine after rebuilding as an A8 class 4 – 6 – 2T, No 69881 eases its train into Sandsend
on 13 July 1957.   *(J C W Halliday)*

An Ivatt 2 – 6 – 0 crossing Sandsend Viaduct and entering the Station with a Middlesbrough train in Summer 1957. *(N E Stead collection)*

A8 No 69879 crossing Newholm Beck Viaduct with a Middlesbrough to Scarborough train in the mid 1950s. *(N E Stead collection)*

The North Yorkshire & Cleveland Railway

An almost new 77010 shunting at Potto about 1956. The staggered up platform is hidden by the train. The main building survives, as does the weighbridge hut bearing an authentic sign "All coals to be paid for on delivery". Otherwise, the entire site is now occupied by Prestons of Potto.   *(J F Sedgwick)*

Popularly know as the Esk Valley Line, the inland route from Teesside to Whitby began as the North Yorkshire & Cleveland Railway. Authorised in 1854, the NY & CR was promoted jointly by the Leeds Northern Railway with which it was to connect at Picton, and the West Hartlepool Harbour & Railway Company. As with most other lines in Cleveland, the main attraction was the prospect of traffic in ironstone. The Leeds Northern was one of the constituent companies which amalgamated on 31 July 1854 to form the North Eastern Railway which took over full control of the NY & CR in 1859.

The line from Picton to Stokesley opened on 3 May 1857 together with the two mile branch from Potto to Swainby which was soon turning out two train loads of ironstone per day. The Swainby branch survived until 1892.

The railway was extended to Ingleby on 1 February 1858 and through Battersby to Kildale on 6 April. Castleton was reached on 1 April 1861 but it took until 2 October 1865 to complete the route to Grosmont on the Whitby and Pickering line. Meanwhile a branch had opened in 1864, initially only for goods, from Battersby to Nunthorpe Junction on the Middlesbrough-Guisborough line. A passenger service between Middlesbrough and Battersby commenced in 1868.

For much of its life, the Esk Valley line enjoyed a modest passenger service beginning with four trains per day in each direction. By 1910 the number had

risen to five with departures from Whitby at 7.00 and 10.11am, 1.30, 3.05 and 5.50pm. All ran to Stockton via Picton apart from the first train in the morning which reversed at Battersby and continued to Stockton via Middlesbrough but there was a connection via Picton which reached Stockton only eight minutes after the main train.

The Esk Valley line suffered a setback on 23 July 1930 when a stone bridge was demolished by the swollen River Esk in Arncliffe Woods just east of Glaisdale. Traffic was suspended between Glaisdale and Egton until 25 May 1931 when a replacement girder bridge was opened using the old abutments. After only three months use, this too collapsed during floods which swept away one of the abutments leaving the new girder to fall into the river bed. This time a new pier was sunk into the middle of the river and the existing girder was re-erected to reach from there to the bank on one side whilst a similar girder was built to cover the other span. The route reopened for the second time on 27 August 1932 and the bridge has caused no trouble since. In view of the closures which took place on neighbouring lines around 1930 and with an alternative route then available via the coast, the Esk Valley line was fortunate to survive this period.

The 1950 summer timetable shows five departures from Whitby via the Esk Valley at 6.45am, 12.00 noon, 4.00, 5.50 and 8.30pm. Only the 6.45am and 5.50pm ran to Stockton via Picton with

ROBIN HOODS BAY

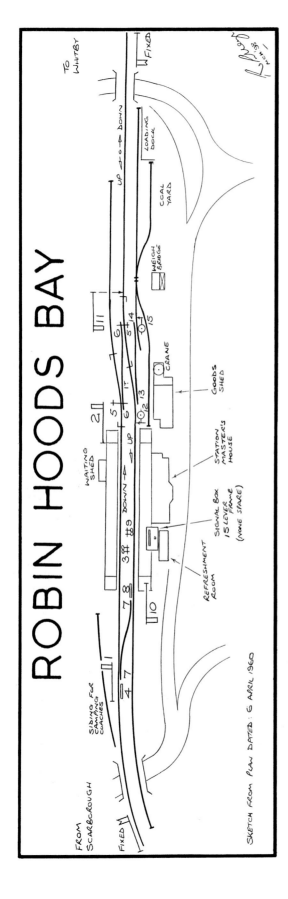

SKETCH FROM PLAN DATED: 6 APRIL 1960

BATTERSBY

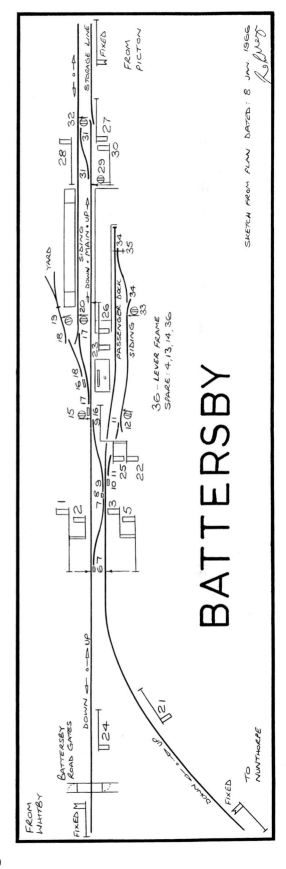

36 - LEVER FRAME
SPARE: 4, 13, 14, 36

SKETCH FROM PLAN DATED: 8 JAN. 1966

40

L1 No 67754 ready to leave Battersby for Middlesbrough 26 April 1958. From the following month, the diesels would make the reversal operation a lot easier. *(J C W Halliday)*

Glaisdale, viewed from a train departing for Whitby in 1958. It is still a passing place but the signal box was closed in 1989. *(J C W Halliday)*

Trenholme Bar looking towards Picton in 1958. The level crossing is with the A19 road which is very busy today.
(Alan Young collection)

Stokesley about 1905. The station was a mile south of the town. The main building still stands.
(Martin Bairstow collection)

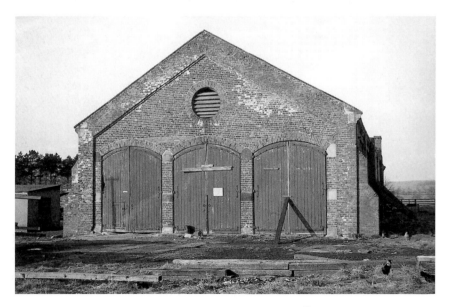

Battersby Engine Shed was built in 1876 to assist the movement of iron ore. When this traffic declined, the shed closed on 30 November 1895. It stood another 70 years, seeing little use except to store withdrawn locos and, during the First World, as a refuge for six dining saloons.
(Martin Bairstow collection)

On 16 January 1950, Commondale became the first station in the area to be converted to an unstaffed halt.
(D Butterfield)

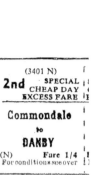

A Metro Cammell DMU leaving Danby for Whitby in 1966. The signal box had latterly served only as a ground frame for the goods yard, closed the previous year. It had once controlled a passing loop but, in the absence of a second platform, had never been allowed to pass two passenger trains.
(D J Mitchell)

Lealholme on 6 March 1965.
(Geoffrey Lewthwaite)

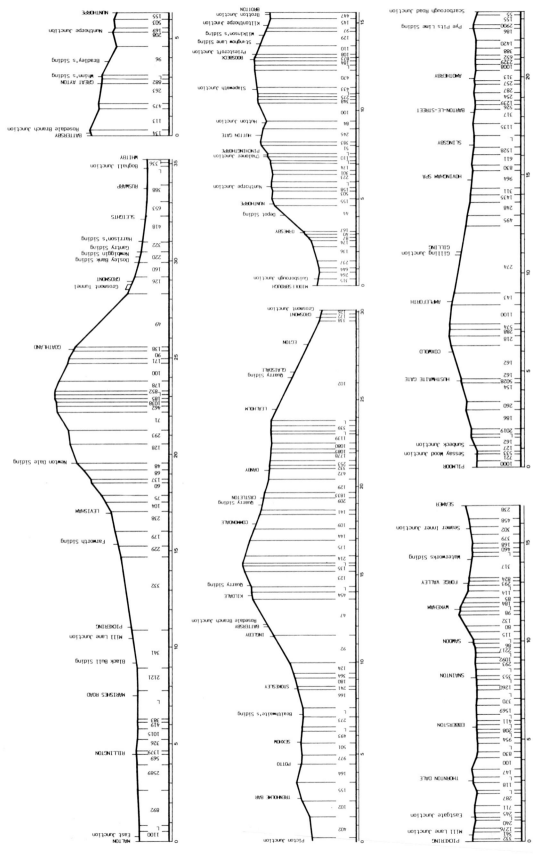

44

Between 1862 and 1891, the landscape at Grosmont was dominated by the ironworks. The site is now the National Park car park.
(Frank Meadow Sutcliffe)

connections at Battersby for Middlesbrough. The other three workings reversed at Battersby to reach Middlesbrough. In the opposite direction, there were three trains from Stockton to Whitby via Picton plus a fourth involving a change at Battersby into one of the two through trains from Middlesbrough. This meant that the Picton to Battersby section had four trains eastbound but only two the other way. The two Sunday trains in each direction ran to and from Middlesbrough via Nunthorpe.

In June 1954, the passenger service was withdrawn west of Battersby and all trains then had to reverse. From May 1958 this operation was rendered a great deal easier with the introduction of diesel multiple units. In the first summer following closure of the coast route these offered up to 15 workings each way between Middlesbrough and Whitby.

A journey along the surviving Esk Valley route is described later. The closed section between Picton and Battersby was double track but from the early 1940s all traffic was worked on the eastbound line west of Ingleby, the other one being given over to wagon storage. At Ingleby westbound trains had to draw forward from the station and then set back across a trailing cross-over before continuing the journey along the 'wrong-line' which was regulated on the staff and ticket system.

From Picton, the branch used to swing south east to Trenholme Bar, a remote station on the Stockton to Thirsk main road. A climb past Black Horse Crossing led to Potto where the platforms were staggered. The principal station was Stokesley where the annual show would bring up to a dozen specials for passengers and quite a few laden with livestock. From Stokesley the line continued to climb towards the Cleveland Hills and Battersby.

Freight traffic ceased west of Stokesley in November 1958 but the line was still used between Picton and Trenholme Bar for wagon storage until 1971. Stokesley closed at the end of July 1965.

The Cleveland Extension Mineral Railway
The building of ironworks at Glaisdale in 1868 prompted the promotion of a 10¼ mile line which would have run across the moors starting at Lingdale Junction, south of Brotton, and joining the Esk Valley route about ¾ mile north west of Glaisdale Station.

The railway was incorporated by an Act of 7 July 1873 and some earthworks were completed before the premature closure of Glaisdale Ironworks in 1876. The railway company tried to press ahead emphasising the potential for mining ironstone in the area through which the line was to have passed. It came to nothing.

The mileposts between Battersby and Grosmont are measured from Picton, which closed on 2 January 1960. 47368 passes the remains on 3 January 1984.
(Alan Young)

The NY & CR joined the Whitby & Pickering at Grosmont where the signal box stood in the angle between the two routes. *(J C W Halliday)*

```
 3rd · SINGLE      SINGLE · 3rd
         Great Ayton To
   Great Ayton          Great Ayton
   Kildale              Kildale
        KILDALE
         via Battersby
   (N)    0/9    Fare   0/9    (N)
 For conditions see over  For conditions see over
```

Rosedale Iron Ore

A view from inside the two road engine shed at Rosedale, built in 1861 and demolished in 1937.

(R Hayes, courtesy Charles Allenby)

The small village of Rosedale Abbey is today virtually the only sign of permanent life in this isolated valley through which the River Seven flows from its source at Rosedale Head towards Ryedale. In the mid nineteenth century, Rosedale was the source of rich ironstone deposits which caused the North Eastern Railway to construct 19 miles of line to connect both East and West Rosedale with its own system at Battersby.

The 14 mile route from Battersby to West Rosedale was authorised by the North Yorkshire & Cleveland Act of July 1858 and opened on 27 March 1861. Curving sharply away from the NY & CR at Battersby, where there was a small marshalling yard, the branch ran in an almost straight line on a rising gradient until, after 2½ miles it reached the foot of the Ingleby Incline.

1430 yards in length, the incline started at 1 in 11 but the gradient increased to 1 in 5 towards the top. It was double track unlike the rest of the branch, and loaded wagons going downhill, usually three at a time, were counterbalanced by empty ones going up.

From the incline top, the branch followed the 1,000ft contour employing numerous curves to avoid the adjoining deep, steep sided valleys.

At Blakey Junction, the East Rosedale branch trailed in so that traffic had to reverse direction. 4¾ miles in length, the branch was built by the mine owners at East Rosedale but taken over by the NER which opened it on 18 August 1865. The line headed north to Rosedale Head then required fairly heavy earthworks to curve round and descend to the level of the mine workings.

An engine shed was built at West Rosedale for the opening of the branch. In the early years of the twentieth century, up to five ex Stockton &

Darlington 0-6-0s were based at Rosedale hauling ironstone from both termini to the incline top. After 1919 their place was taken by three J24 locos, Nos. 1860, 1893 and 1950. All routine maintenance was carried out at Rosedale Shed. If an engine required to be moved off the branch its centre wheels had to be removed before it could be lowered down the incline.

General goods traffic on the branch was minimal and there was never any passenger service though railway and mining families travelled on the goods trains. The method of working above the incline was staff and ticket with three sections divided at Blakey Junction where there was a man to make sure that the drivers had the correct authority. There were no signals.

The ironstone output reached a peak in 1873. Six years later the mines were closed. They reopened on a number of occasions but never reached the same level of activity. They closed finally in 1926.

The last commercial traffic over the railway was the waste product of the calcining kilns. This was all removed by January 1929 after which demolition commenced. Rosedale Shed closed on 24 January when two of its three engines were transferred to Saltburn. Track and other materials were carried out by rail until the last locomotive (No. 1893) was lowered down the incline on 8 June 1929.

For working traffic onwards from the incline bottom to the blast furnaces on Teesside, a three road engine shed was built at Battersby in 1876. By that time, the ironstone traffic was already past its peak and the shed closed in 1895. It remained standing for a further 70 years during which time it saw various uses mainly storage. During the First World War it housed some restaurant cars but was empty for many years before demolition in 1965.

J24 class 0 – 6 – 0 No 1860 with a train for Rosedale at Bloworth Crossing, about 1 mile south of the incline top.

(R Hayes, courtesy Charles Allenby)

No 1860 at Sledge Shoe, one mile beyond Blakey Junction, heading towards West Rosedale.

(R Hayes, courtesy Charles Allenby)

The Lastingham & Rosedale Light Railway

In 1896 legislation was passed aimed at facilitating the construction of light railways in rural areas. A light railway is not actually defined in the Act. Low speed would be as good an explanation as any because the Act imposed a speed limit of 25 miles per hour in return for relieving some of the obligations on fencing and level crossing protection. Most important the need for a special Act of Parliament for each railway was replaced by a Light Railway Order from the Board of Trade (Later the Department of Transport).

Most light railways promoted around the turn of the century came to nothing. Such a scheme was the Lastingham & Rosedale which would have run from Sinnington to Rosedale Abbey. An agreement was signed with the NER for a junction with the Gilling to Pickering line at Sinnington where the light

railway would have had its own station across the road from that of the NER.

Intermediate stations were to have been provided at Appleton-Le-Moors, Lastingham and Hartoft. It was hoped also to have a connection with the NER Rosedale West branch so as to permit the direct movement of goods to the Middlesbrough area. The promoters even ventured to suggest that their line would become part of a through route for passengers between Scarborough and the North. They undertook to operate the light railway with their own locomotives, rolling stock and staff rather than seek a working agreement with the NER believing their method to be 'more economical'.

Their confidence proved to be ill founded. Although some preliminary work was carried out, the scheme fell by the wayside.

The Scarborough & Whitby Railway

The 1865 curve at Rillington and the short lived through service from Scarborough to Whitby may have been an NER response to counter the threat of a direct railway along the coast. If this was the case then the early withdrawal of the NER service may indicate that the company quickly recognised that a coastal line was going to take a considerable time to achieve.

An Act incorporating the Scarborough & Whitby Railway was passed in July 1865. The authorised line would have left the NER west of Scarborough, and rejoined it between Sleights and Ruswarp. The necessary capital could not be raised and the scheme failed.

The 1871 a new Act was granted for a more modest scheme. This was to be an isolated line starting from Gallows Close in Scarborough which was separated by high ground from the NER main line. At Whitby the line was to descend by a 1 in 5½ incline to a terminus on the south side of the Esk.

The necessity of linking up with the NER was recognised in a further Act passed in May 1873 which authorised the connecting tunnel at Scarborough and the substantial Larpool Viaduct which would carry the line to join the proposed Whitby, Redcar & Middlesbrough Union Railway at Prospect Hill. At this stage work at the southern end of the line was progressing but little else then happened during the remainder of the 1870s.

A fresh Act of 1880 revived the earlier powers and this time work did get under way leading eventually to the opening of the railway on 16 July 1885. By an agreement signed the previous year, the line was worked by the NER in return for half the receipts. As was usually the case with such arrangements, there was continued dispute with the owning company accusing the NER of failing to exploit the line fully and the NER responding with complaints about the standards of construction and maintenance of the railway. In 1898 this matter was brought to an end when the NER purchased the Scarborough & Whitby Railway for less than half what it had cost to build.

An exterior view of Scarborough Station about 1906. Part of it dates from 1845 but the clock tower was added in the 1880s. The trams operated between May 1904 and September 1931. No 13 is going to the West Pier.
(Peter E Baughan collection)

Dieselisation in evidence at Scarborough in August 1961.
(Peter Sunderland)

Platform 1A was cut out of the extremity of platform 1 to give easier access to the Whitby line. *(Peter Sunderland)*

Errata Volume Two

Two errors crept into the captions for Scarborough line photos in the first (1996) edition of *Volume Two.* On page 35, 69885 is entering Whitby West Cliff with the 11.40 Scarborough to Middlesbrough in August 1957. On page 96, 42085 is at the north end of West Cliff. The signal is clear for the connecting Middlesbrough to Scarborough train.

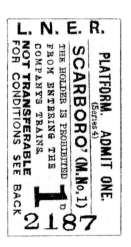

The entrance to Falsgrave Tunnel, seen from the end of platform 1A in August 1961. *(Peter Sunderland)*

Scarborough goods depot was at Gallows Close, north of Falsgrave Tunnel. J72 class 0 – 6 – 0T No 69016 shunts the yard on 4 September 1952.
(John Oxley)

J25 No 65690 approaching Scarborough with a pick up goods from Whitby on 6 September 1952. The train is on the single track Whitby line. The other track leads independently from North-stead Carriage Sidings.
(N E W Skinner)

Metro Cammell DMUs for Scarborough and Middles-brough passing at Cloughton, early in 1965.
(D J Mitchell)

The exterior of Cloughton Station, restored and extended in 1996. Holiday accommodation is offered in the station, in a mark 1 camping coach and, from 2008, in the former goods shed. There is also a tea room.
(Martin Bairstow)

Hayburn Wyke looking north about 1900. The platform had been on the other side of the track from 1885 until reconstruction in 1893, using the same buildings.
(Peter E Baughan collection)

A DMU from Scarborough pauses at Stainton Dale before resuming the climb towards Ravenscar and Whitby, early in 1965.
(D J Mitchell)

The Scarborough & Whitby was a difficult line to work in bad weather. On the morning of 19 January 1959, a combination of mist and sea fret made the rails so greasy that the service was virtually halted all day. There had been no trains on the previous day, a Winter Sunday. The first southbound working on the Monday, the 7.28am from Middlesbrough was formed of a 3 car dmu. After coming to a stand near Hawsker, it returned to Whitby where the centre trailer was removed but, even with just the two power cars, it fared no better. It was a design fault of the dmus that they had no sanding equipment although on this occasion the steam locos did not do much better.

Class D49 4-4-0 No. 62751 was sent out from Scarborough to assist but could not make any progress with the diesel whose passengers were eventually taken to Scarborough by road arriving mid afternoon instead of 9.58am.

The next service from Whitby at 11.20am was worked by 2-6-4T No. 42084 with two coaches. 62751 was attached as pilot at Robin Hood's Bay but the train stalled on the climb to Ravenscar and after running out of sand returned to Whitby.

The first northbound train left Scarborough at 12.52pm over an hour late with D49 No. 62770 and two coaches. It failed to restart from Stainton Dale and had to leave one coach there. After struggling on to Robin Hood's Bay it again stuck on the 1 in 43 leaving that station. No. 62751 came from Whitby to assist and eventually the two D49s brought their single coach into Whitby at 4.40pm. They then returned light engine to Scarborough sanding the rails in advance of the six o'clock dmu which was able to follow. Further sanding was carried out by steam locomotives overnight.

The *Whitby Gazette* records an 'unanticipated and unwelcome' delay to an excursion train returning to Scarborough on the evening of Saturday 19 October 1889. 'When the train had nearly reached Peak (Ravenscar), it was found that the engine was not powerful enough to pull the train up the heavy gradient'. The article is rather non-technical but it seems that the train had to be banked up to Ravenscar by the locomotive off the following ordinary passenger train. The excursion then reached Scarborough 'about an hour late' whilst the ordinary train, due at 8.52, did not put in an appearance until 10.10pm.

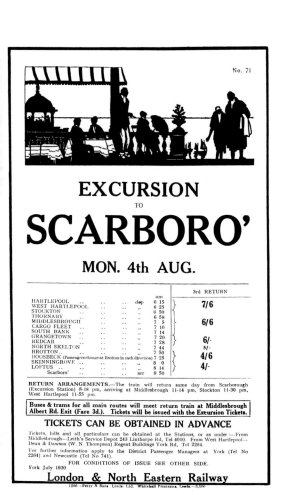

British Railways were evidently keen to avoid such incidents with the 'scenic excursions' which they ran over the Malton–Whitby–Scarborough lines hence the double heading on the accompanying photographs.

The Special Traffic Notice for Sunday 12 August 1956 shows 'scenic excursions' from Harrogate and Bradford Forster Square running about half an hour apart. The Harrogate train arrives at Whitby Town via Pickering at 12.41, leaves at 3.12 reversing at West Cliff, arrives at Scarborough 4.38 and leaves there at 9.00pm. The Bradford train has a shorter stay at Whitby. It arrives at 1.02pm, leaves at 2.35,

reverses at Prospect Hill, reaches Scarborough at 4.04 and departs for home at 8.10pm. Both trains are double headed from Whitby Town to Ravenscar where the assisting engines are detached. They leave Ravenscar at 4.30pm as two light engines coupled together reaching Whitby Town at 5.11pm after reversal at Prospect Hill.

During the final years of the Scarborough and Malton routes, scenic excursions were run by dmus which could offer passengers a much better view. In the peak season of 1959 from 6 July, an excursion ran daily from Scarborough to Whitby, out via Pickering and back by the Coast.

The gradient is apparent as a Metro Cammell set pulls into Stainton Dale, bound for Middlesbrough early in 1965.
(D J Mitchell)

A fine study of a NER slotted post signal as Ivatt 2 – 6 – 2T No 41265 pilots a B1 on a southbound excursion on 12 July 1959. (John Oxley)

The 2.20pm Scarborough to Whitby approaching Stainton Dale in August 1957 behind 2 – 6 – 4T No 42084. *(M Mitchell)*

The Station Master at Stainton Dale exchanging tablets with the driver of a Scarborough bound DMU. *(Martin Bairstow collection)*

The "Whitby Moors Rail Tour" pulls away from Stainton Dale on the last day of the Scarborough to Whitby line. *(D J Mitchell)*

A southbound train entering Ravenscar prior to the building of the passing loop and second platform in 1908.
(Martin Bairstow collection)

Ravenscar never developed. From 1890, building plots were sold and roads laid out. A brickworks with a rail siding opened north of the tunnel to meet anticipated demand but the terrace in Station Square was all that materialised.

The 7.10 Scarborough to Darlington at Ravenscar behind B1 No 61224 on 2 September 1952.
(John Oxley)

Ravenscar looking south. Originally named Peak, the station was closed for 12 months from March 1895 because the Scarborough & Whitby Company would not build a house for the NER Station Master.
(Geoffrey Lewthwaite)

The 10.45am Middlesbrough to Scarborough climbs towards Ravenscar on 7 August 1957, hauled by Ivatt 2 – 6 – 0 No 43057.   (M Mitchell)

On the same day, the 11.40 Scarborough to Middlesbrough emerges from Ravenscar Tunnel behind class A8 No 69867.   (M Mitchell)

The south portal of Ravenscar Tunnel, 279 yards in length. The tunnel is not part of the present day cycle track.
(D Ibbotson)

Class A6 No 692 at Robin Hoods Bay with a train for Scarborough about 1939.
(Martin Bairstow collection)

Hawsker Station in 1958.
(Geoffrey Lewthwaite)

The guard gives the signal to restart a Scarborough to Middlesbrough train from Hawsker. The van body used as a store is so permanent that it supports an oil lamp. Hawsker Station is now used for holiday accommodation and cycle hire.

(J C W Halliday)

B1 No 61083 passing Prospect Hill with a train from Middlesbrough to Scarborough. The line to Whitby Town drops down under the box, whose starter signal is positioned up the embankment for sighting.

(Martin Bairstow collection)

Ivatt 2 – 6 – 0 No 43051 has crossed Larpool Viaduct and is approaching Prospect Hill with the 2.57pm express from Scarborough, first stop West Cliff then all stations to Brotton and non stop to Middlesbrough. The late running 2.20pm all stations Scarborough to Whitby Town can be seen disappearing towards Bog Hall having reversed at West Cliff. *(A M Ross)*

A Metro Cammell unit climbing up from Whitby Town towards Propect Hill, where it will reverse then pass over Larpool Viaduct.
(Martin Bairstow collection)

The Ryedale Lines

Class V2 No 60879 between Husthwaite Gate and Sunbeck with the 10.25 Saturdays only Scarborough Glasgow on 18 August 1962. *(M Mitchell)*

Gilling Station was the focal point of a small network of lines serving the predominantly agricultural district in the angle between the East Coast Main Line and the York–Scarborough route. The first section to be built was authorised in 1847 as the Thirsk & Malton Railway. It was a branch of the York, Newcastle & Berwick Railway starting not at Thirsk itself but at Pilmoor, six miles to the south. Progress was slow in the difficult years following the end of the 'Railway Mania' but under pressure from the independent Malton & Driffield company, the YN & BR pressed ahead.

Under the 1847 Act, the T&M would have run direct into Malton by means of a junction with the Scarborough line just east of the station. Instead, an amending Act of 1852, authorised the T&M to cross over the Scarborough line and to make its junction with the Malton & Driffield Railway so as to provide a direct route from the North towards Driffield.

Both the T&M and M&D Railways opened on Thursday 19 May 1853 when the ceremonial opening train left Pilmoor at midday. Pausing at Hovingham to engage in some mutual congratulation and at Slingsby for luncheon, the train reached Driffield at 2.30. It then returned to Malton where guests were treated to 'a most sumptuous repast'.

The line then settled down to an everyday existence with three passenger trains daily running between Pilmoor and Malton.

The mid 1860s saw an upsurge in the scale of railway promotion which was to lead eventually to the completion of the branch from Gilling to Pickering. The NER was concerned at a threat to its territorial monopoly contained in proposals by the London & North Western Railway for new lines to Teesside and to Scarborough.

In its Yorkshire New Lines Act of 1866, the NER attempted to put an end to speculation by building its own duplicate route from Leeds to Scarborough via Wetherby, Knaresborough, Boroughbridge, Pilmoor and Malton. As mentioned in 'Railways Around Harrogate' (Volume One), only the Cross Gates to Wetherby and Knaresborough to Boroughbridge lines, conceived as part of this plan, were eventually built. In contrast the proposed improvements between Pilmoor and Malton line never came to anything.

South of Pilmoor, a bridge was built across the York to Darlington main line so as to join the Boroughbridge and Malton branches but no track was ever laid. Nor was double track provided between Pilmoor and Malton. Nor was any work

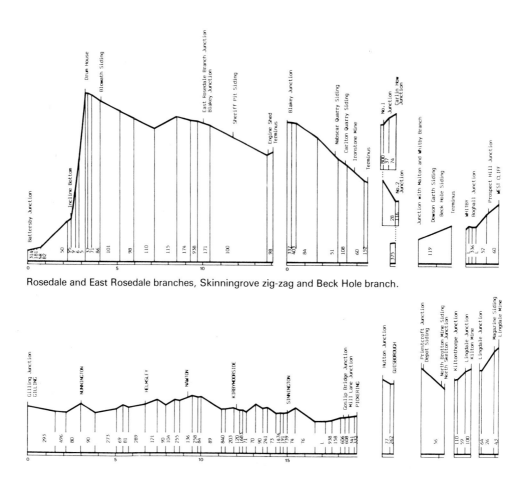

Rosedale and East Rosedale branches, Skinningrove zig-zag and Beck Hole branch.

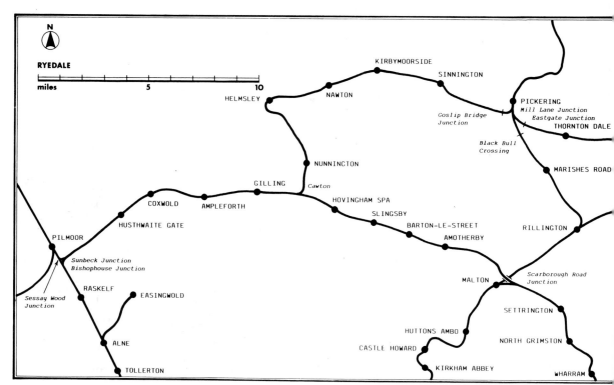

carried out on a proposed 2½ mile 'cut off' north of Malton which would have given direct running towards Scarborough.

The associated scheme for a branch from Gilling to Pickering, also authorised in 1866, proved more fortunate. Again, as recorded in 'Railways Around Harrogate' a number of schemes approved in the mid 1860s had to be abandoned when the trade cycle began to take its downward turn at the end of the decade. The NER contemplated terminating the proposed branch from Gilling at Helmsley. Instead by an Act of 1869, the route into Pickering was altered so as to approach the town from the south and avoid the 400 yard tunnel east of Sinnington which would have been required under the original proposal to join the Whitby line near New Bridge.

The branch was opened in three stages: Helmsley was reached on 9 October 1871, Kirbymoorside on New Years Day 1874 whilst the remaining section to Mill Lane Junction, Pickering opened on 1 April 1875. The curve between Bishophouse and Sunbeck Junctions south of Pilmoor opened on the same day as Helmsley and was eventually to facilitate through running between York and Pickering.

It was the practice of the NER, that where a single track branch joined a double track main line, the branch would itself become double for a short distance so as to form a conventional double track turnout at the junction. Thus both curves from the main lines at Pilmoor were double track but at Sunbeck Junction they converged into a single line. The sections from Sunbeck to Coxwold and from Coxwold to Gilling were the first on this route to be converted to electric token working from 15 March 1902.

At Husthwaite Gate, the station house, which is still occupied, was set back from the line on the Pilmoor side of the level crossing. The single platform was at the Gilling side and the points and signals were operated from an elevated ground frame. The first passing loop was at Coxwold, a

B1 class 4 – 6 – 0 No 61289 rounds the double track curve from Pilmoor South (Sessay Wood) and is about to enter the single track at Sunbeck Junction. The corresponding curve from Bishophouse Junction was also double track.
(J W Hague, courtesy David Beeken)

Sunbeck Junction box seen from a passing brake van in 1957.   *(J C W Halliday)*

more substantial station with the main buildings on the north side and the signal box on the opposite platform.

Ampleforth Station was a mile and a half from the village at a very remote location. It closed in 1950 but still required to be manned for the level crossing and signals which were controlled from a small hut.

In recognition of Gilling's status as the junction between the Pickering and Malton lines, it was provided with a footbridge in 1894, the only such installation on these lines. In a bid to avoid confusion, Gilling carried the suffix 'For Ampleforth College' since this establishment was nearer to Gilling than it was to Ampleforth Station. From 1895 until the 1920s, a 2ft gauge tramway was employed to carry goods the 1½ miles from the College Siding at Gilling to the school itself. The track ran alongside the mainline for more than half a mile then climbed steeply up the hillside.

The Malton and Pickering routes left Gilling as two single lines. For nearly 1¾ miles, the railway appeared to be double track but there was no junction at Cawton where the two lines simply diverged.

Between Hovingham and the outskirts of Malton, the railway ran parallel to the B1257 road but about half a mile to the north and each of the four stations were on the edge or even some way beyond their respective villages. Barton-le-Street was particularly remote.

The goods yard at Hovingham Spa was enlarged in 1948 to accommodate quarry traffic which was being despatched in up to three train loads per day until 1960 to steelworks on Teesside. Slingsby was a passing loop but with only one platform. Its distinguishing feature was a three storey goods warehouse. Main traffic at Amotherby was the Corn Mill built in 1862 alongside the station.

There were further level crossings and attendant cottages at Swinton, Broughton and Pasture Lane. A quarry siding was opened at Pye Pitts near Old Malton in 1856 but disappeared before the Second World War. The River Derwent was crossed by a three arch steel viaduct. Trains from Gilling crossed over the York-Scarborough Line to join the Driffield line at Scarborough Road Junction. Here they reversed direction to enter Malton Station by a double track curve.

The route to Pickering parted company with the Malton line at Cawton and immediately turned through 90 degrees. The first station at Nunnington is now a hotel and restaurant. The village of Harome never merited a passenger station but a siding was provided about ¾ mile from the village to facilitate the delivery of coal and the despatch of sugar beet. The small community at Harome Siding comprised four railway cottages housing the crossing keeper and plate layers.

Helmsley Station lay on the tight curve which took the railway from a north westerly to an easterly coast. The dominating feature was the glass verandah which protected travellers from the elements on the main (Pickering bound) platform.

During the First World War a siding was laid from Helmsley goods yard to the Waterloo Plantation some three miles to the west for the extraction of timber.

The largest engineering feature on the branch was Kirkdale Viaduct which crossed the Hodge Beck about a mile beyond Nawton Station. Built of stone, the three arch structure still stands.

The guard shuts the gates behind the pick up goods at Hovingham in 1957. When occasional passenger trains ran, station masters had to arrange attendance at level crossings, many of which were normally crew operated.
(J C W Halliday)

Opposite page upper The last passenger train to cross the three arch Kirkdale Viaduct, between Nawton and Kirbymoorside, was a ramblers' excursion from Bradford Forster Square on Sunday 3 May 1964.
(G W Allenby)

Lower English Welsh & Scottish Railway No 56095 with a train of loaded potash between Skinningrove and Brotton on 25 June 2003.
(G W Morrison)

J27 class 0 – 6 – 0 No 65844 heading east through Gilling with a mixed freight in August 1961.

(M Mitchell)

Kirbymoorside Station now belongs to the farm machinery firm of Russell's which occupied land adjacent to the railway from the 1920s and was one of its customers. In 1930 a quarry siding was installed on the north side of the line at Spaunton midway between Kirbymoorside and Sinnington just east of Catter Beck level crossing. The siding was last used in February 1948 when a locomotive was derailed on it.

Sinnington Station was a very similar structure to Kirbymoorside but without the passing loop and additional platform. Immediately on leaving Sinnington, the line passed through Riseborough Cutting the largest earthwork on the branch. There were a further four level crossings on the descent from Riseborough at Aislaby Carr, Costa Beck, Westgate Carr and Goslip Bridge. Until 1924 Goslip Bridge Junction marked the end of the single line but on 24 February, the block post there was abolished and the curve was singled round to Mill Lane Junction were the Malton to Whitby line was joined half a mile south of Pickering. This move coincided with the conversion of the block section from Kirbymoorside from staff and ticket to electric token operation.

The passenger service between Malton and Gilling fell victim at the end of 1930 to a policy by which the LNER abandoned certain lightly used trains in favour of its associated bus companies. The four intermediate stations remained open for goods and still booked passengers for the occasional excursion. A similar fate had befallen all the local stations on the main York to Scarborough line the previous September.

A service of four trains per day continued in each direction between York and Pickering. In the 1938 summer timetable there was an additional lunch time working from Pickering to Gilling and back operated by a Sentinel car which came through from Scarborough along the Forge Valley line. In addition there was an unadvertised train from Helmsley in the morning during term time only taking the children to school in Pickering with a corresponding return trip in the afternoon. By 1950 thee were just three trains between York and Pickering, one of which later became Saturdays only, plus the school train.

The last day of normal service was Saturday 31 January 1953, a day which is better remembered for the severe flooding in East Anglia and the tragic loss of the 'Princess Victoria' between Stranraer and Larne. The 6.00 pm departure from York was in the care of class D49 No. 62735 'Westmorland". At Coxwold it passed No. 62730 'Berkshire' on the last up service. Small crowds braved the elements to witness the progress of the train at each station. Arrival at Pickering was punctual at 7.53. After a brief ceremony in which the Pickering Station Master broke a bottle over the engine to declare the line closed, mourners adjourned to the 7.40 Malton train which had been held specially to allow them to get back to York.

Only the Kirbymoorside–Pickering section closed

An excursion does reasonable business at Hovingham on 28 April 1963.
(Geoffrey Lewthwaite)

The last rush hour at Gilling, Monday 27 July 1964. The six car train on the right headed by the Cravens set is the 8am from Helmsley to Scarborough which ran non stop from Gilling apart from the double reversal at Malton.. The seven car train on the left is the 8.39 from Gilling which called at Hovingham, Slingsby, Barton Le Street and Amotherby en route to Scarborough. Both trains were Sunday school excursions and were the last passenger workings on the line. (Charles Allenby)

J27 No 65681 coming off the Gilling line at Bishophouse Junction with a southbound goods on 7 June 1950. The East Coast Main Line was then only three tracks at this point. The up slow line was not laid between Pilmoor and Alne until 1959. (Chris Wilson)

completely. The remainder of the route continued in use for freight and excursions. Gilling even retained a booking office at which Mr Charles Allenby worked between August 1961 and February 1964. The station normally came to life on six days per year when a special train ran to or from Kings Cross carrying pupils for Ampleforth College at the start and end of each term. A second train, in later years a dmu, ran from Leeds.

A couple of days before the end of term, Mr Allenby used to visit the college to affix parcels stamps on to the boys' trunks which were to be loaded into five vans for different destinations which would be delivered to the College Siding at Gilling. The booking office retained a rack of Edmondson card tickets just as at a normal open station. At other times of year, tickets were issued for travel from York usually to customers connected with the College. Tickets could be issued for any journey on BR but in those days there was no national fares manual and the fare had to be obtained in York.

Other passenger movements after 1953 included ramblers excursions, bringing people from the West Riding to stations on the branch. In the other direction there were occasional special trains taking people from Kirbymoorside, Helmsley etc. on, for example, day trips to Scarborough organised by local Sunday Schools. Each summer until 1962, the route between Pilmoor and Malton was used by through trains on Saturdays between the North East and Scarborough. These workings brought prestige motive power through Gilling in the form of 4-6-2 'Pacific' steam locomotives and latterly class 40 diesels. These trains were pulled back from Scarborough Road Junction to Malton Station and vice versa by a loco from Malton Shed whilst the train engine remained at the other end.

Until 5 February 1962, a stone train ran from Thirsk via Gilling and Malton to the quarry at Thornton Dale on the remaining stub of the Forge Valley line. This doubled up as the pick up goods for Coxwold and Husthwaite Gate. After this train ceased, those two stations were served if required by the Malton to Kirbymoorside pick up. This meant that Sunbeck Junction went for weeks on end without seeing a train. By that time the curve from Pilmoor was single track and the one from the south had been lifted. The box boasted three operational levers: a home signal each way plus a direction lever controlling the tokenless block from Pilmoor.

The signalman had to open up in case the pick up required to go to Husthwaite Gate which possibly happened once or twice per week. He would then accept the train from Coxwold where the signalman could then issue the token to the driver who would return it after propelling back from Husthwaite Gate to Coxwold. At this time the entire railway between Malton, Kirbymoorside and Pilmoor remained operational albeit normally for the sole use of the goods which did not run every day and not necessarily for the full length of the line. One or two of the remote level crossings had become unmanned though they were attended by platelayers if passenger trains ran. It was at this point that Dr Beeching arrived on the scene to pronounce the end of the entire operation.

An accident on the main line at Pilmoor damaged Sessay Wood Junction in the early hours of 19 March 1963. It was not repaired and the line was cut back to Husthwaite Gate. The last Ampleforth College specials ran on 28 April 1964. A ramblers excursion on 3 May proved to be the last passenger train to Nawton and Kirbymoorside. Then on Monday 27 July two Sunday School excursions, of six and seven coaches respectively, ran from Helmsley and from Gilling to Scarborough. At the end of the following week, on Friday 7 August 1964, the pick up goods made its last trip behind class J27 0-6-0 No. 65894 which was brought in specially. Normally the working had been in the care of a diesel shunter since the closure of Malton shed in April 1963. A contract with the Corn Mill at Amotherby delayed closure of the final section from Malton by just ten weeks until 16 October.

Coxwold looking towards Pilmoor in 1957.
(J C W Halliday)

B1 No 61274 negotiates the level crossing at the west end of Coxwold Station with the 8.40am (Saturdays only) Scarborough to Glasgow on 9 August 1958. *(M Mitchell)*

Scarborough Road Junction on 15 August 1961 with class J27 No 65844 in charge of a freight from the Gilling line. The signal box is the original, 1862 structure, which was replaced in 1873 by a tall box from which the signalman could see over the road bridge. *(M Mitchell)*

A J27 0 – 6 – 0 ambles through Nunnington with a modest payload on 5 August 1958.   (M Mitchell)

J27 No 65844 shunting at Helmsley on 27 August 1959.   (M Mitchell)

B1 No 61021 "Reitbok" passing Helmsley with a railtour on 1 October 1963.
(D J Mitchell)

Latterly, the thrice weekly pick up was worked by a class 03 diesel. It is seen heading east from Helmsley.
(Charles Allenby)

D20 No 62387 running round a railtour at Kirbymoorside, then the end of the line, on 2 June 1957. *(J Davenport)*

The Forge Valley Line

The popular name for this long forgotten byway was that of one of its stations. The railway did not run through the Forge Valley but crossed it in the village of West Ayton. Possibly to avoid confusion with Great Ayton, near Battersby, the station there was known as Forge Valley.

The Forge Valley Railway was actually the official name of a proposed line which reached the stage of an aborted Parliamentary Bill in 1873. This would have run north from West Ayton, through the Forge Valley itself before curving round to join the embryonic Scarborough & Whitby Railway just south of Scalby Station.

When the North Eastern Railway eventually opened the line from Pickering in 1882, it approached Scarborough from Forge Valley Station by going south via Seamer. Here it joined the main line from York just west of its junction with the Bridlington line.

Seamer Station was and still is an island platform. In 1911 a loop was installed on the north side of the layout from Seamer Junction rejoining the mainline at the level crossing end of the station. This line was provided with a platform (No. 1) linked by a footbridge to the island which became platforms 2 and 3. The loop was accessible by trains from Pickering, York or Bridlington which could stand in platform 1 and be overtaken. It was not, however, capable of use by trains from Scarborough to Pickering as might seem logical nowadays. Reversible working only became acceptable in comparatively recent times. Access to the Forge Valley line was by a conventional double track junction. The line then singled a little way along the branch.

At the other end, the Forge Valley joined the Malton to Whitby line at Mill Lane just south of the junction with the line from Gilling. Again the turnout was originally double as far as Eastgate Junction. Later this was abolished and the single track began at Mill Lane. Here trains for both Gilling and Scarborough crossed over onto the 'wrong' line which was reversible for a short distance over the level crossing before the two branches diverged in opposite directions.

Between its two junctions, the Forge Valley line was single track regulated by electric key tokens. There was just one passing place, Snainton. There was a standard design of station building all of which survive in various uses. The gradient was easy with only short stretches steeper than 1 in 100. The line served an agricultural community and enjoyed five trains in each direction in the period before the First World War.

Sentinel railcars were employed from 1928 giving a slightly better frequency of service. The Summer 1938 timetable shows seven journeys each way. There was never a Sunday service on this as on many other north Eastern branches.

Unfortunately the line depended heavily on local traffic. It was hardly a through route and most of the stations were consistently further away from their villages than the parallel road. The last train was push-pulled out of Scarborough by Class G5 No. 67273 at 6.40pm on Saturday 3 June 1950. This marked complete closure of the line except for the section west of Thornton Dale which was retained for quarry traffic until 1963.

The quarry at Thornton Dale kept open the truncated line from Pickering until 1963. G5 No 67315 trundles through the station on 7 August 1957. The station is now used as holiday cottages.   *(M Mitchell)*

A8 class 4 – 6 – 2T No 1502 passing Snainton with a train of empty stock for Scarborough in 1936. The station is now a garage doing MOT repairs and bodywork.
(Charles Allenby collection)

The stations on the Forge Valley line were all of a standard design and all are still standing. This is Ebberston looking towards Scarborough. It now offers holiday accommodation in three mark 2 carriages.
(Martin Bairstow collection)

Sawdon also looking towards Scarborough. The lady is standing in front of the hut which houses the ground frame. Sawdon has also found a new use as holiday accommodation.
(Martin Bairstow collection)

Autocars and Railcars

BTP class 0 – 4 – 4T No 87 sandwiched in the middle of the 2.42pm "autocar" from Middlesbrough to Saltburn via Guisborough and Brotton ascending Nunthorpe Bank on 24 April 1919. The additional vehicles in the rear will come off at Guisborough.
(LCGB Ken Nunn collection)

The first use of the word "autocar" on the North Eastern Railway was in respect of the two petrol electrics, Nos 3170 and 3171. These entered service in 1904, one between Scarborough and Filey, the other between West Hartlepool and Hartlepool. The body of No 3170 survived as a holiday home and is now at the Embsay & Bolton Abbey Steam Railway as a long term restoration project.

The petrol electrics were possibly 50 years ahead of their time. The NER did not persevere with internal combustion technology. When it wanted a larger fleet of "autocars", it opted to stay with steam.

The BTP (Branch Tank Passenger) locos were designed by Edward Fletcher, Chief Mechanical Engineer of the NER, in 1873. 124 were built. Some survived into the LNER period, becoming class G6. From the late 1890s, they began to be replaced on local passenger work by the NER class O (LNER G5). Some of the BTPs were rebuilt as 0 – 6 – 0Ts, becoming class J77. Of those which remained 0 - 4 – 4Ts, about 37 were push – pull fitted from 1905. Together with some clerestory roof compartment coaches, these became steam autocars.

The make up of an autocar was either a loco and driving trailer or two driving trailers with the loco sandwiched in between. When a carriage was leading, the driver had control of the regulator and reverser by means of rods under the carriage body. He had a Westinghouse brake, a hand brake, a whistle and a speaking tube for communication with the fireman on the engine. An autocar did not carry a guard.

Autocars were noted in the public timetable, not as a selling point, but as a warning that accommodation for luggage was limited. Only the petrol electric cars were third class only. Steam autocars had first class compartments. Their principal use was on short passengers journeys which didn't carry much van traffic, such as Middlesbrough to West Hartlepool, Billingham to Port Clarence and Hull to Brough.

In 1910, the entire service of ten trains a day between Middlesbrough and Guisborough was rostered for autocars. Most of these continued to Brotton, Loftus or Saltburn. The 2.47 and 4.52pm from Middlesbrough ran all stations to Saltburn via Brotton, taking 1 hour 6 minutes with four reversals. Two of the six daily trains between Saltburn and Whitby were autocars. In mid summer, these will have been replaced by conventional trains, releasing the autocar for the Beckhole service. There were no autocars advertised between Middlesbrough and Eston in 1910 but two out of the four daily trains were autocars in 1918.

The Sentinel – Cammell Steam Cars

In 1923, Sentinel Wagon Works of Shrewsbury supplied a steam railcar for the narrow gauge Jersey Railway. The body came from Cammell Laird at Nottingham. The following year, Sentinel – Cammell produced a standard gauge version for the Wembley Exhibition. The LNER agreed to a trial. The first offering was found to be underpowered so a larger boiler was fitted for a second trial. This involved a visit to Whitby to assess performance on gradients. The result was an order for two cars, Nos 12E and 13E which entered service in May 1925.

Two heavier cars were built in 1927. One of these, No 22, was given a test run on 6 April between York and Whitby, out via Pickering and back via Scarborough. Between Whitby and Robin Hoods Bay, it hauled a horse box. It then entered traffic at Heaton (Newcastle) whilst No 21 went to Botanic Gardens (Hull). An order was placed for 20 more, delivered in the first half of 1928. The engine compartment was articulated onto the passenger coach.

Although the two cylinder car had managed a trial trip to Whitby, the LNER was looking for something more powerful to work on steeply graded lines with a tail load. The manufacturers obliged with a six cylinder 200hp car, mounted in a single rigid body. No 2135 "Integrity" was unique in having a rigid body but still a two cylinder engine. The ultimate development came with the twin engine 12 cylinder version and the solitary power car and trailer multiple unit.

A summary of the 80 vehicles built for the LNER is as follows;

2 lightweight two cylinder	1925
22 articulated two cylinder	1927 -28
1 rigid two cylinder	1928
49 rigid six cylinder	1928 - 31
5 rigid 12 cylinder	1930-32
1 12 cylinder twin car	1930

Because of the need to replace BTP autocars, more than two thirds of the Sentinels went to the former North Eastern Railway. Two cylinder No 237 "Rodney" took over the Forge Valley service in April 1928.

No 2281 "Old John Bull", the first 12 cylinder car, built in June 1930, was allocated to Middlesbrough. Its sister, No 2283 "Old Blue" went to Guisborough where it replaced Class F8 No 685. This had been the sole resident at Guisborough since withdrawal of the last BTP, No 1436 in July 1929. The two cars worked to Brotton, Loftus and Saltburn and Battersby, making several ascents of Nunthorpe Bank each day.

In October 1931, the LNER Board considered a proposal to purchase four further 12 cylinder Sentinel cars for the coast line between Scarborough, Whitby and Saltburn. These would provide the entire service for nine months of the year. There would have to be a reduction in the number of winter trains between Whitby and West Cliff. It was proposed that one car be based at Scarborough, one at Saltburn and two at Whitby, one of which would be a spare. The project would save money by not having to employ guards and through lower operating costs, even after allowing 5% interest on the capital outlay.

The Board decided to order three cars but defered a decision on the fourth. Nos 220 "Defence", 246 "Royal Sovereign" and 248 "Tantivy" were delivered towards the end of 1932. They were the last Sentinel cars built for the LNER. They were slightly longer than their predecessors with an extra row of seats. But with superior seating, they managed four seats on each row rather than five, giving a capacity of 48.

"Tyneside Venturer"

The question of the fourth car was decided when the LNER purchased the 250hp diesel electric "Tyneside Venturer". Built by Armstrong Whitworth, it began trials on the LNER in November 1931. On 11 April 1932 it entered service in the Newcastle area, still owned by Armstrong Whitworth. After six months, it was transferred to Middlesbrough for the Guisborough and Saltburn service, upon which it proved both reliable and popular.

The Divisional General Manager (N E Area) reported that "the travelling public prefer the Diesel to the Sentinel steam coach, particularly on account of the absence of smoke steam and flying sparks." The capital cost was almost double that of a Sentinel but it was hoped that this would be offset by lower running costs, especially fuel consumption. "Tyneside Venturer" entered LNER stock in January 1933.

In summer, railcars were inadequate for the coastal service, which then reverted to loco hauled operation. "Tyneside Venturer" worked a daily excursion at 10am from Scarborough to Whitby, out via Forge Valley and Pickering, returning in the afternoon via Robin Hoods Bay. The Sentinels worked additional summer journeys between Whitby and Goathland and provided connections at

No 25 "Tyneside Venturer".
(Martin Bairstow collection)

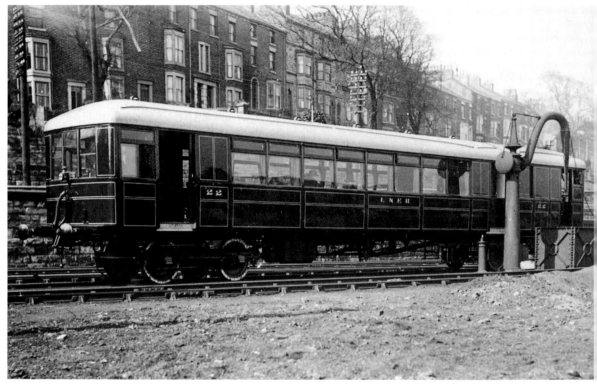

Resplendent in varnished teak, No 22 reposes at Whitby during a break in its trial run on 6 April 1927. It was later given the name "Brilliant" and repainted in green and cream.　　　　　*(H G W Household)*

For the next stage of the journey, a horse box was added to test No 22's hauling capacity. It is seen on arrival at Robin Hoods Bay.

(H G W Household)

Opposite page upper G5 No 67343 has just left Sleights with a local for Malton in March 1954. 110 examples of this class were built between 1894 and 1901. The last was withdrawn in 1958. There is a project to build the 111th member of the class.

(J M Jarvis/ Colour-Rail)

Lower Class B1 No 61018 "Gnu" with the pick up goods at Sleights in May 1964. The guard is armed with a shunting pole with which to disconnect the loose couplings during the shunting operation.

(J M Boyes/ Colour Rail)

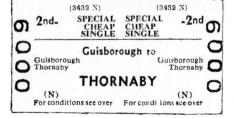

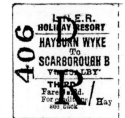

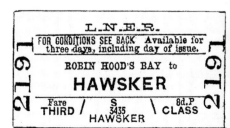

West Cliff to and from Whitby. These latter workings sometimes involved two Sentinels coupled together, each with its own crew.

The winter 1935-6 depot allocations included;

Guisborough	2283	"Old Blue" (12cyl)
Malton	2236	"British Queen" (6cyl)
Middlesbrough	2281	"Old John Bull" (12cyl)
	25	"Tyneside Venturer" (D)
Saltburn	267	"Liberty" (2cyl)
Scarborough	220	"Defence" (12cyl)
Stockton	2139	"Hark Forward" (6cyl)
	2231	"Swift" (6cyl)
	2232	"Alexander" (6cyl)
	2235	"Britannia" (6cyl)
Whitby	2219	"New Fly" (6cyl)
	246	"Royal Sovereign" (12cyl)
	248	"Tantivy" (12cyl)

The Malton car worked the Forge Valley line, beginning and ending with a passenger turn from Malton to Pickering and back. The Stockton cars had duties north of the Tees as well as to Battersby,

Guisborough and Whitby. The Saltburn car ran mainly to Brotton.

Apart from No 220 "Waterwitch", destroyed in an accident near Doncaster in 1929, all the Sentinels survived up to the outbreak of war in September 1939. With the reduction in local train services, some were withdrawn but those in best condition were stored at Darlington. Some of these came back into traffic as other cars failed. All were scrapped either during, or immediately after the war. No 248 "Tantivy", the last to be built was first to be scrapped in September 1939. It had covered 146,000 miles in just under seven years. Last to go was No 2136 "Hope" in February of 1948.

No LNER, or other contemporary Sentinel car was preserved. However, the Buckinghamshire Railway Centre, at Quainton Road has a three car articulated set built by Sentinel and Metro Cammell for Egypt in 1951.

No 25 "Tyneside Venturer" suffered declining reliability and was withdrawn in 1939, having

Two cylinder No 265 "Neptune" at Brotton in 1937, probably on the Saltburn service.

(Martin Bairstow collection)

A Sentinel car entering Grosmont Tunnel en route from Goathland to Whitby about 1936. *(D Ibbotson)*

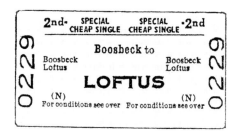

```
2nd- SPECIAL    SPECIAL ·2nd
       CHEAP SINGLE  CHEAP SINGLE
0229          Boosbeck to          0229
      Boosbeck              Boosbeck
      Loftus                Loftus
            LOFTUS
      (N)                     (N)
      For conditions see over  For conditions see over
```

Winter Service 1938-39

These are departures Mondays to Fridays from Middlesbrough for Nunthorpe and beyond between 26 September 1938 and 30 April 1939. All were rostered for Sentinel cars or "Tyneside Venturer"

5.58am	Loftus
6.25	Scarborough
7.28	Battersby
7.42	Guisborough
8.33	Guisborough
9.33	Guisborough
10.03	Scarborough
10.33	Battersby
11.33	Guisborough
12.03pm	Guisborough
12.33	Scarborough
1.03	Guisborough
1.33	Guisborough
2.03	Battersby
2.33	Scarborough
3.33	Brotton
4.43	Battersby
5.03	Guisborough
5.33	Guisborough
6.03	Whitby via Loftus
6.28	Whitby via Battersby
7.03	Guisborough
8.03	Loftus
8.33	Battersby
9.33	Guisborough

covered about 250,000 miles. The same fate befell the other two Armstrong Whitworth diesels, No 224 "Lady Hamilton" and No 232 "Northumbrian". It is unlikely that they received adequate maintenance on an almost 100% steam railway. It would have made more sense to have concentrated all three at one depot covering the same group of services. The LNER seems to have abandoned its initial enthusiasm for diesel technology.

It was not until well after the Second World War, that dieselisation began on a serious scale. After experimenting with some prototypes, British Railways introduced their first production series Diesel Multiple Units in 1954. They reached the Whitby area in 1958, taking over the Middlesbrough to Scarborough service from Monday 5 May, the day that all services were diverted via the Esk Valley.

No 248 "Tantivy" at Goathland about 1936.   (Martin Bairstow collection)

The Saturday service was identical, except that the 9.33pm went through to Loftus and there was a 11.10pm to Guisborough. There was no Sunday service in Winter.

All trains for Brotton and beyond called at Guisborough apart from the 10.03am. Passengers from Guisborough towards Scarborough could change onto this train at Hutton Gate. The 3.33pm connected for Loftus at Brotton.

Passengers from Middlesbrough could also reach Brotton by changing at Saltburn. There were nine services a day (ten Saturdays) between Saltburn and Brotton.

The Battersby trains gave reasonable connections both to Stokesley and Whitby, except that the 4.43pm connected only in Whitby direction and the 8.33pm only for Stokesley.

The four Scarborough trains travelled via Loftus but did not serve Whitby Town. Only the 10.03am had a connection at West Cliff.

In Summer, there were additional trains to Scarborough at 8.03, 9.15 and 11.33am, 1.33 and 4.33pm. The 6.03pm went to Scarborough rather than Whitby and the 8.03pm was extended from Loftus to Scarborough. The 9.33pm went to Loftus every weekday. None of the Scarborough trains served Whitby Town but almost all had connections at West Cliff. There were additional journeys between Saltburn and Brotton so as to connect with most of the Scarborough trains. Some of the Summer only trains missed various intermediate stations.

On Summer Sundays, there were nine trains from Middlesbrough to Scarborough, most leaving at 3 or 33 minutes past the hour. All but one served Guisborough but none had connections from West Cliff to Whitby Town. There was only one train between West Cliff and Whitby on a Sunday, even in Summer. There were however three trains from Middlesbrough to Whitby via Battersby, where they were allowed 10 minutes to run round. There were no Sunday trains between Picton and Battersby but the Saltburn to Brotton service did function on Summer Sundays.

There were one or two extra trains to Scarborough running on individual Summer Saturdays from places on Teesside according to works holidays. Some of these reached Brotton via Saltburn Junction, rather than Nunthorpe.

It was some time before the next generation of railcar emerged in the mid 1950s. A Metro Cammell DMU at Guisborough.   *(Martin Bairstow collection)*

Train Services along the coast

When the WR & MU line first opened, the trains operated between Saltburn and Whitby Town but it was only a year and a half until the Scarborough line came into use. Then some trains ran through from Saltburn to Scarborough leaving Whitby Town Station to be served by a shuttle service to and from West Cliff.

In 1910 there were six trains daily in each direction between Saltburn and Whitby and five between Whitby and Scarborough. Some ran right through with connections to and from Whitby Town whilst others ran from Saltburn to Whitby Town and from Whitby Town to Scarborough connecting with each other at West Cliff. Two of the Saltburn–Whitby workings were advertised as 'autocars' but not any of the trains to Scarborough. There were short workings from Cloughton to Scarborough four times per day.

The Summer 1922 timetable shows six trains virtually at the same times leaving Saltburn but a couple of short workings have appeared between Hinderwell and Whitby Town. There are slightly more trains between Whitby and Scarborough whilst some of the Cloughton trains are extended to and from Stainton Dale. The only Sunday service comprises four return trips from Scarborough to Stainton Dale presumably worked by an 'autocar' but that edition of 'Bradshaw' does not specify.

By the Summer of 1932, the short workings had gone. There were still six departures from Saltburn very similarly timed with seven trains on the Whitby–Scarborough section. On Sundays there were just three trains in the afternoon between Whitby Town and Scarborough.

For the summer of 1933, the northern terminus was changed from Saltburn to Middlesbrough. All trains travelled via Nunthorpe and Guisborough where longer trains were permitted to propel in and out of the station aided by a board proclaiming the word 'seven' at the point where the driver of a 7 coach train should stop his engine. In later summers some trains were routed via Redcar.

There were five through trains between Middlesbrough and Scarborough plus two in the evening between Middlesbrough and Whitby and an additional morning one from Whitby to Scarborough. There were still three Sunday trains but only south of Whitby.

Most departures from Middlesbrough were at 3 or 33 minutes past the hour to fit in with the pattern of Sentinel railcar departures. The combined service to Guisborough was virtually half hourly during the day but with some gaps.

The traffic responded to the changes more than the trains could cope and extras had to be run. In 1934 the service was increased to give nine through trains each way plus the first through Sunday service.

Operation at Scarborough was rendered much easier by the cutting of a bay platform (No. 1A) into the extremity of platform 1. Propelling out of the main part of Scarborough Station to Falsgrave Junction was only permitted with up to two coaches. Longer trains had to depart with the engine at the front and then stand on the main line whilst it ran round before heading off into Falsgrave Tunnel. Traffic on the other routes into Scarborough was also busy and this operation was stretching capacity in the congested station area. From platform 1A, trains of up to five coaches could set off with the engine at the buffer stop end, set back a short distance and then go into forward gear as soon as clear of the points at Falsgrave Junction. The arriving trains could propel into platform 1A. The only snag was that passengers had to walk the length of platform 1 to reach the Whitby train which used to wait three minutes after the advertised departure time to give everybody a chance to catch it. This time it would then make good by the easier manoeuvre compared with departing on time from one of the other platforms.

Further increases in the numbers of trains were made in the following summers. Consideration was given to providing Fyling Hall and Hawsker Stations with second platforms so that two passenger trains could cross there. A passenger train, even one advertised non stop, was not allowed to stand at a passing station if there was no platform. Stations with loops but no second platform could only pass a passenger and a freight or two freight trains. These alterations might have taken place if the Second World War had not put a stop to this passenger boom.

As a guide to the frequency of trains over the coast route, a list of departures from the two Whitby Stations is given for the peak Summer of 1938. There were of course additional excursion and relief trains. It was a problem that the Summer timetable lasted only ten weeks and the railway had to operate way below capacity for most of the other 42 weeks in the year.

After the war, intensive peak services were gradually restored. In 1950 there were 14 trains on a Summer Saturday from Middlesbrough mostly going through to Scarborough. The 8.28am (SO) stopped only at Kettleness, West Cliff and Stainton Dale and took 2 hours 27 minutes for the 58 miles. Stopping trains took around three hours. Some trains left Middlesbrough via Redcar. The Monday to Friday service was less frequent. There were six trains from Middlesbrough on a Sunday all between 9.15am and 1.20pm and returning at half hourly intervals from Scarborough in the evening.

In Winter the service was restricted to three trains each way on weekdays only. Without the shuttle service between the two Whitby Stations only a few Middlesbrough–Scarborough trains had connections to Whitby Town. In 1955 this was partly remedied when operating regulations were relaxed to permit trains of up to two coaches to propel between the Whitby Town, Prospect Hill and West Cliff. Some trains then ran from Middlesbrough to Scarborough via West Cliff and Whitby Town being propelled back to Prospect Hill. Trains starting from

With daffodils on the embankment, 2 – 6 – 4T No 80117 heads away from Staithes with the 11.40 Scarborough to Middlesbrough on 18 April 1958.   *(A M Ross)*

Later the same day, class L1 No 67765 comes off the viaduct with the 4.20pm Middlesbrough to Scarborough.   *(A M Ross)*

To Scarborough

	Town	West Cliff
	6.45 am	6.56 am
	—	8.24
	(9.15)	9.31
	(9.54)	10.07
	(10.30)	10.50
	—	11.21
	(11.25)	11.42
	—	12.16 pm
SO	12.30 pm	12.44
	(1.15)	1.28
SO	—	1.54
	(2.08)	2.20
	(3.05)	3.24
	(4.10)	4.23
	(6.02)	6.21
	(7.25)	7.51
	(9.38)	10.00
MThSO	10.20	10.36

Sundays

	Town	West Cliff
	—	10.07 am
	—	10.50
	—	11.21
	—	11.42
	—	12.16 pm
	—	12.53
	—	1.28
	—	1.54
	—	2.19
	—	3.24
	—	4.19
	6.57	7.08
	—	9.58

To Middlesbrough

	Town	West Cliff
	7.14 am	7.22 am
	(9.15)	9.35
	(10.30)	10.49
	(12.30) pm	12.55 pm
	(2.08)	2.32
	(3.05)	3.35
	(5.15)	5.32
	(6.02)	6.20
	—	6.59
	(7.25)	7.49
SO	—	8.27
	—	8.57
	—	9.27
	(9.38)	9.58
SO	(10.20)	10.38

Sundays

	Town	West Cliff
	—	12.56 pm
	—	3.30
	4.45 pm	5.03
	—	5.23
	—	6.36
	—	6.59
	(6.57)	7.19
	—	7.49
	—	8.18
	—	8.51
	—	9.27
	—	9.56
	—	10.34

To Malton etc

	Town	
	7.07 am	Malton
MFSO	8.00	Malton
	9.20	Goathland
	9.40	Kings Cross
	10.00	Malton
	10.35	Goathland
	11.15	Malton
SO	11.45	Leeds
	12.10 pm	Leeds
SX	12.40	Goathland
SO	12.50	Goathland
	1.32	Malton
	2.15	Goathland
	2.45	Malton
	3.53	Malton
	4.25	Goathland
SO	6.05	Leeds
	7.00	Malton
	9.10	Goathland

Sundays

Town	
1.55 pm	Kings Cross
2.15	Goathland
4.00	Grosmont
5.06	Goathland
6.52	Goathland
7.35	York
7.50	Leeds
8.10	Goathland

Esk Valley

	6.54 am	Middlesbrough (Stockton)
	7.25	Glaisdale
	10.10	Stockton (Middlesbrough)
SO	12.35 pm	Glaisdale
	1.20	Stockton (Middlesbrough)
	3.38	Castleton
	5.47	Stockton (Middlesbrough)
	6.25	Glaisdale
	8.12	Stockton (Middlesbrough)
SX	9.25	Glaisdale
SO	9.25	Middlesbrough

Sundays

Town	
6.35 pm	Middlesbrough
8.36 pm	Middlesbrough
9.10 pm	Middlesbrough

Connecting trains in brackets

SO	Saturdays Only
SX	Saturdays Excepted
MThSO	Mondays, Thursdays and Saturdays Only
MFSO	Mondays, Fridays and Saturdays Only

```
              L. N. E. R.
0341   FOR CONDITIONS SEE BACK  Available for   0340
       three days, including day of issue
          HAYBURN WYKE to
             RAVENSCAR
        Fare   /    S    \  7d.0
       THIRD      3228      CLASS
               RAVENSCAR
```

Whitby Town for Scarborough could propel all the way to West Cliff at 10mph then set off for Scarborough without running round.

In 1958 BR blamed the cost of maintaining the viaducts for the decision to close the line between Whitby and Loftus.

The coming of the diesels

The demise of the railway, along the coast from Whitby to Loftus was recalled by Stuart Carmichael in the opening chapter. A sad day no doubt but one not entirely without consolation. From the following Monday, 5 May 1958, an enhanced service was introduced on the alternative Esk Valley route between Middlesbrough, Whitby and Scarborough employing diesel multiple units. For the first time all trains served Whitby Town Station.

The new trains were only marginally faster than the old. The dmus were able to make lighter work of the four reversals at Battersby, Whitby Town, West Cliff and Falsgrave but on some journeys the schedules were stretched for example by standing eight minutes at Castleton Moor so as to suit the times of trains coming the other way. Average journey time for the 58½ miles through journey was 2 hours 40 minutes which was about the same as that previously achieved by the steam trains using the coast route if they served both stations in Whitby.

On a route better noted for its scenic qualities than for speed, the diesel trains had the considerable advantage in giving passengers a much improved view including the possibility of travelling immediately behind the driver. Generally this sought after position was first class at one end of the Metro Cammell set and second class at the other.

Another opportunity afforded by the diesels was that of issuing tickets on the train and dispensing with staff at some of the little used wayside stations. This was difficult with non gangwayed coaches. Fyling Hall became unstaffed the day the diesels started.

By 1962 staff had also been withdrawn from Hayburn Wyke, Commondale, Kildale, Great Ayton and Hutton Gate Stations but that was as far as the process got before a much larger bombshell hit the Railways Around Whitby.

The majority of Malton to Whitby trains became dmu operated from 6 April 1959 when both Pickering and Whitby engine sheds closed. The

Some steam working remained. A scenic excursion, from Bradford Forster Square on 10 July 1960 is double headed on the Whitby to Scarborough leg with 2 – 6 – 4T No 42085 piloting B1 No 61198. 42085 is preserved on the Lakeside & Haverthwaite Railway. *(N E W Skinner)*

A Middlesbrough to Scarborough DMU entering Robin Hoods Bay, early in 1965. The main building now offers holiday accommodation. In mid summer 1959, a DMU ran a daily scenic excursion from Scarborough to Pickering, Whitby and back via the coast. *(D J Mitchell)*

An attraction of the first generation DMUs was the view ahead through the driver's cab. Entering Hayburn Wyke on 6 March 1965. *(Geoffrey Lewthwaite)*

5.20am from Malton and the evening departure from Whitby remained steam hauled along with their corresponding return workings because of the volume of mail and parcels. These were the responsibility of Malton Shed until that closed in April 1963. For a year steam locos were provided by York Shed but the workings were taken over by class 40 diesels during 1964.

The 1958 closure had only effected four intermediate stations on the coast between Whitby West Cliff and Loftus. Initially both these places benefitted from the new diesel trains but the Loftus service was cut back to Guisborough in May 1960 and Whitby West Cliff closed just in time for the Summer season in June 1961. After that trains to and from Scarborough reversed at Prospect Hill Junction.

The summer 1962 timetable is reproduced for one direction only between Scarborough, Whitby and Middlesbrough, Guisborough and Middlesbrough and between Whitby, Malton and York. All the trains were diesel multiple units except on the Whitby to York service where there was a mixture of steam and diesel. At that time, the North Eastern Region timetable identified dmu services as this was considered a selling point. There were additional excursion trains over and above the timetabled service.

While there were gaps in the Whitby to York service, passengers sometimes had the option of going via Scarborough. Between 21 July and 1 September 1962 there was a connection off the 7.54pm Whitby to Scarborough arriving York at 10.12pm. It was also possible to leave Whitby for York on a Sunday at 9.20am, 12.35 or 4.22pm changing at Scarborough but the journey took longer than via Pickering and probably involved a higher fare.

In Winter, which lasted from September to June the service was less extensive. There were just five trains between Middlesbrough and Whitby with four going on to Scarborough. Five trains linked Malton and Whitby and there were the morning and lunchtime locals between Whitby and Goathland. There were no Sunday trains outside of the Summer period.

Most of the trains had changed from steam to diesel by 1959. But in 1974, Ruswarp station was still in the age of the gas lamp. *(Alan Young)*

A Metro Cammell unit calls at Sleights on its way to Whitby, about 1964. *(Charles Allenby)*

Weekdays	am	am	am	am	SX am	SO am	pm	pm	pm	pm	pm	pm	pm..	pm	SO pm		Sundays	am	am	pm	pm	pm	pm	pm	pm	pm
SCARBOROUGH CEN				10.23	11.25	11.52	2.05	2.44	4.35	5.04			6.11	7.08	7.55			10.33	2.33		5.11	5.45	6.11	7.16	7.39
CLOUGHTON				10.39	11.46	12.07	2.20	3.00	4.54	5.19			6.27	7.23	8.10			10.49	2.49		5.30	6.00	6.26	7.31	7.54
HAYBURN WYKE				10.43	11.52		2.24	3.04	4.58				6.31	7.27				10.53	2.53			6.04	6.30		7.58
STAINTON DALE				10.46	12.00	12.13	2.27	3.07	5.01	5.25			6.34	7.30	8.16			10.56	2.56		5.36	6.07	6.33	7.37	8.01
RAVENSCAR				10.53	12.07	12.20	2.34	3.14	5.08	5.36			6.41	7.37	8.27			11.03	3.03		5.43	6.14	6.40	7.44	8.08
FYLING HALL				11.00	12.14		2.41	3.21	5.15	5.43			6.48		8.34										
ROBIN HOODS BAY				11.08	12.22	12.29	2.45	3.25	5.19	5.47			6.52	7.47	8.38			11.12	3.12		5.52	6.23	6.49	7.57	8.17
HAWSKER				11.16	12.30	12.37	2.53	3.33	5.27				7.00	7.55	8.46										
WHITBY TOWN a				11.31	12.44	12.51	3.07	3.46	5.40	6.06			7.13	8.08	8.59			11.31	3.31		6.11	6.42	7.08	8.16	8.36
WHITBY TOWN d	6.55	9.20	10.30	11.40		12.55		4.03	5.45	6.15	6.50	7.20	8.20			9.15		10.23	11.40		5.45	6.20	6.50	7.20	8.20
RUSWARP	6.58	9.23	10.33	11.43		12.58		4.06	5.48	6.18	6.53	7.23	8.23			9.18		10.26	11.43		5.48	6.23	6.53	7.23	8.23
SLEIGHTS	7.02	9.27	10.37	11.47		1.02		4.10	5.52	6.22	6.57	7.27	8.27			9.22		10.30	11.47		5.52	6.27	6.57	7.27	8.27
GROSMONT	7.10	9.35	10.45	11.55		1.10		4.18	6.00	6.30	7.05	7.35	8.35			9.30		10.38	11.55		6.00	6.35	7.05	7.35	8.35
EGTON	7.14	9.39	10.49	11.59		1.14		4.22	6.04	6.34	7.09	7.39	8.39			9.34		10.42	11.59		6.04	6.39	7.09	7.39	8.39
GLAISDALE	7.19	9.45	10.55	12.05		1.20		4.26	6.10	6.40	7.15	7.45	8.45			9.38		10.55	12.05		6.10	6.45	7.15	7.45	8.45
LEALHOLM	7.24	9.50	11.00	12.10		1.25		4.31	6.15	6.45	7.20	7.50	8.50			9.38		11.00	12.10		6.15	6.50	7.20	7.50	8.50
DANBY	7.32	9.57	11.07	12.17		1.32		4.38	6.22	6.52	7.27	7.57	8.57					11.07	12.17		6.22	6.57	7.27	7.57	8.57
CASTLETON MOOR	7.38	10.08	11.18	12.28		1.38		4.41	6.28	7.03	7.30	8.00	9.00					11.18	12.20		6.28	7.00	7.30	8.00	9.00
COMMONDALE	7.42	10.12	11.22	12.32		1.42		4.45	6.32	7.07	7.34	8.04	9.04					11.22	12.24		6.32	7.04	7.34	8.04	9.04
KILDALE	7.49	10.19	11.29	12.39		1.49		4.52	6.39	7.14	7.41	8.11	9.11					11.29	12.31		6.39	7.11	7.41	8.11	9.11
BATTERSBY	7.58	10.27	11.37	12.47		1.57		5.00	6.47	7.22	7.49	8.19	9.19					11.37	12.39		6.47	7.19	7.49	8.19	9.19
GREAT AYTON	8.04	10.33	11.43	12.53		2.03		5.06	6.53	7.28	7.55	8.25	9.25					11.43	12.45		6.53	7.25	7.55	8.25	9.25
NUNTHORPE	8.12	10.41	11.51	1.01		2.11		5.14	7.01	7.36	8.03	8.33	9.33					11.51	12.53		7.01	7.33	8.03	8.33	9.33
ORMESBY	8.16	10.45	11.55	1.05		2.15		5.18	7.05	7.40	8.07	8.37	9.37					11.55	12.59		7.05	7.37	8.07	8.37	9.37
MIDDLESBROUGH	8.22	10.51	12.05	1.11		2.23		5.24	7.11	7.46	8.13	8.43	9.43					12.01	1.05		7.14	7.46	8.14	8.43	9.43

Guisborough Branch

Weekdays only	am	am	am	am	SX pm	SO pm	pm	SX pm	pm
GUISBOROUGH	7.30	8.12	8.30	9.55	1.30	1.45	4.30	5.42	6.10
HUTTON GATE	7.34	8.16	8.34	9.59	1.34	1.49	4.34	5.46	6.14
NUNTHORPE	7.40	8.22	8.40	10.05	1.40	1.55	4.40	5.52	6.20
ORMESBY	7.44	8.26	8.44	10.09	1.44	1.59	4.44	5.56	6.24
MIDDLESBROUGH	7.50	8.32	8.50	10.15	1.50	2.05	4.50	6.02	6.31

SO   Saturdays Only

SX   Saturdays Excepted

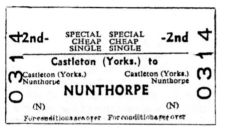

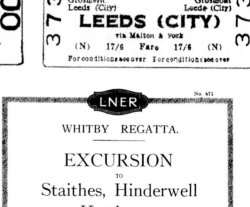

GUISBOROUGH formerly Hutton Junction

DOWN MAIN →

UP MAIN ←

DDLESBROUGH

SKETCH FROM
S.B. DIAGRAM
AS AT 1964

26 Lever C.D Frame
Spare: 21
22/26 Mechanically
worked colour - lights.

GOODS BRANCH

GOODS YARD

← PASSENGER BRANCH →

SPRING

LOCO SHED

STATION GF
No. 20 Release

To BROTTON

STATION

LEVISHAM

NEWTONDALE

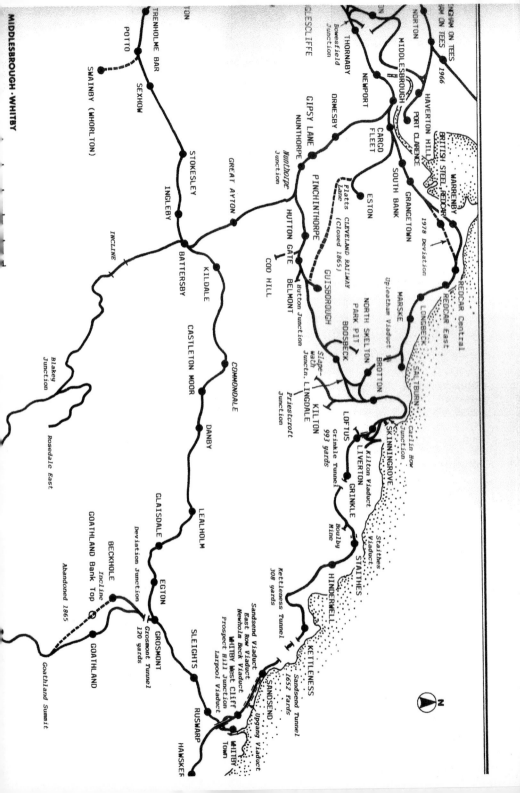

MIDDLESBROUGH · WHITBY

The Sharpening of the Axe

Dieselisation undoubtedly brought a long overdue facelift to the image of the local passenger train – 'a complete break from traditional railway practice ... the sort of thing to bring back business'. (*Trains Illustrated* January 1959). Many services in the North Eastern Region recorded significant increases in patronage.

Unfortunately the substitution of diesel multiple units for steam trains was virtually the only concession to change. In most other respects, the railways continued to operate exactly as before. We now know what scope there was for reducing costs because we have seen it happen on those lines which survived the destruction of the 1960s. We have also seen in recent times how there is scope for the development of rail traffic despite (or even because of) the phenomenal growth of car ownership.

At that time British Railways showed a singular reluctance to shift from a defeatist attitude that operating methods could never be changed and that each stage in the advance of road transport represented a reduction in the role of the railway industry.

Increasing prosperity during the 1950s had been accompanied by growth in personal travel. Although rail traffic had held up reasonably well in absolute terms, as a proportion of a rapidly expanding market, it was in sharp decline. To a growing percentage of an increasingly mobile population, railways were perceived as antiquated, irrelevant to their travel needs and, worse of all, a drain on the taxpayer.

When the railways were nationalised in 1948, it had not been intended that they should be subsidised. Yet after 1952, BR began to incur losses. It was hoped that these would somehow go away and in the meantime they were financed by borrowing, the interest on which created further losses. The programme of piecemeal closures accelerated. Always the choice was between continuing a service exactly as before or stopping it altogether. Economies in operation were not considered.

In 1961, the Government appointed Dr Richard Beeching to take charge of British Railways and to transform it into a viable operation free from subsidy. His brief was to look at the railways in isolation and not to take into account any other social or economic factors.

During 1962, Dr Beeching began to publish a series of incredibly badly drawn maps which purported to show what a small part of the BR network carried the bulk of the traffic. In the summer of that year he announced a moratorium on closure proposals pending the conclusion of his traffic studies. It became obvious that his Report, when published, would contain something far more drastic than had been experienced so far. Nevertheless there was still plenty of complacency in the air right up to the eve of publication in March 1963.

The February 1963 issue of *Modern Railways* predicted that the Report might never be published in full because of the adverse electoral consequences of a programme of major closures. The April edition (which would have gone to press before the Report was published) discussed a suggestion from the Southern Region that stations might become unstaffed as an alternative to closure but concluded that on the whole the idea was impractical. The railway press was evidently more bankrupt even than BR as regards ideas for cheaper methods of operation.

The Beeching Report was duly published at the end of March 1963. It recommended the closure of about half the BR system and promised that these measures, together with a reorganisation of freight traffic to concentrate on goods most suitable to rail movement, would achieve profitability within a period of only a few years. Reduction of costs on loss-making services was not considered, nor was subsidy which Dr Beeching was at pains to stress BR did not want.

When the Report was debated in Parliament in April 1963, the Conservative Government had been in office for 11½ years and would soon be seeking a fourth mandate from the electorate. Surely they would avoid embarking on an unpopular programme particularly one effecting many of their own constituencies. Failing that, surely the opposition would capitalise on the situation by offering an alternative policy. It is a measure of the widespread acceptance of railway closures that the Government pressed ahead and the Opposition did not oppose even though the watered down consultative machinery nicely managed to delay the first impact of closures until the election campaign was in full swing.

The politicians had evidently decided that there was little popular support for the railways. After all the floating voter, who decides the outcomes of elections, was at that time typified by the family which had just bought its first second hand car on hire purchase and thought that trains were the last thing which they would ever need.

Even railway supporters were totally convinced (or maybe demoralised into submission) by the Beeching conclusions. The editorial in *The Railway Magazine* for May 1963 began: 'Whether one agrees with all of "the plan" or not it has to be admitted that Dr Beeching's Report is basically correct and backed by such a weight of carefully prepared evidence as to be almost unassailable. It has been described as brutal, brilliant and right'.

As far as Whitby was concerned, the Beeching Report could not have been more savage. All three routes – to Malton, Scarborough and Middlesbrough – were recommended for closure along with the surviving branch to Guisborough.

Before this could happen, travellers had to be given the opportunity to object to the Transport Users Consultative Committee. Their task was to assemble evidence of hardship and submit this to the Minister of Transport who would then decide whether closure went ahead. His decision was a political one. Ernest Marples was the Minister who had appointed Dr Beeching and was committed to carrying out his recommendations. The majority of his judgements naturally went in favour of closure. The Guisborough service quickly passed through the procedure and closed at the end of February 1964.

Closure notices were published in respect of all three lines to Whitby early in 1964. The normal procedure at the TUCC public hearings was for those travellers who bothered to speak up to protest that their journeys would not be possible by bus and for BR representatives to say that they would. In the case of seaside lines many of the passengers were tourists who travelled only occasionally and were not necessarily resident in the area. They were even less likely to make any effort to contest closure than the daily commuters on other lines. Hoteliers and traders pleaded for their livelihoods and threatened that Whitby would become a 'ghost town' but they were dismissed as a joke. Rising car ownership would surely make good the loss of railway business in only a few years.

Such was the momentum of railway closures by the summer of 1964, that individual cases barely merited a mention even in the railway press. Those contesting the Whitby closures really must have felt that they were fighting a lone battle.

The outcome was reported in the October 1964 edition of *Modern Railways* in the following brief terms. 'After hearing objections to the NER proposals for closure of all passenger services to Whitby, the local TUCC advised the Minister of Transport that in their view hardship would result from withdrawal but only the Middlesbrough–Whitby line has been reprieved'.

The November issue did enlarge on the matter and conceded that the decision to close the Malton to Whitby service was particularly surprising as the TUCC had reported that 'severe hardship' would result at Pickering and at Goathland.

Looking back it was not merely surprising but incredible that the Government did not make a greater concession to Whitby in the middle of a general election campaign. The decision to reprieve the Esk Valley route was a short term expedient because the pick up goods happened to run to Whitby that way. Many people had expected the 'main line' to Malton to be the most likely candidate for survival.

Locally the matter became an election issue. The Labour Party had gone into the campaign with no alternative transport policy other than a vague promise to suspend 'major closures' for further investigation. The Labour candidate for the Scarborough and Whitby constituency produced a written undertaking from Harold Wilson that the two condemned Whitby routes were amongst the 'major closures' covered by the manifesto pledge.

By 16 October, Mr Wilson was in Downing Street. Called upon to redeem his pledge, the new Transport Minister, Mr Fraser, explained that due to a technicality in the 1962 Transport Act, he was powerless to reverse his predecessor's decision even though it had not yet been implemented. Apparently not even the Prime Minister had the authority (or the desire) to request that a nationalised industry should slow down on a matter of public concern. To reinforce the fact that there was to be no change in Government policy, Mr Fraser went on to pronounce judgement in a further 40 outstanding cases ordering closure of all but one.

The December issue of *Modern Railways* reported Mr Fraser's approval of '40 or so' closures without even naming them. It then went onto justify Mr Wilson's broken pledge over Whitby and congratulated the unsung civil servant who had found the 'technicality' in the legislation which had relieved the new Government from having to reverse any closure decisions. Then it devoted almost as many column inches to condemning a threatened increase from 1d to 2d in the charge for using certain station toilets. Not only were closures not opposed they were not even news.

The Conservative MP for Scarborough and Whitby honoured his own pledge by introducing a private members bill under the 'ten minute rule' which is precisely how long it took for that gesture to fizzle out.

It only remained for BR to fix a date for closure of the two routes serving Whitby from the South. On 6 March 1965, ordinary services were supplemented by a 'Whitby Moors Rail Tour' hauled by preserved K4 No. 3442 'The Great Marquess' and K1 No. 62005 which is itself now preserved.

For a couple of years, the North Eastern Region timetable showed replacement buses from Malton and Scarborough to Whitby first with times and then with the more familiar note saying 'bus times not available'. Whitby was listed in the index as a 'place not directly served by rail' with a footnote saying that a rail service was in fact available via Middlesbrough.

Whitby to Malton and York   Summer 1962

Weekdays	D a m	D a m	S X a m	S O a m	S O a m	S O a m	D a m	D p m	S O p m	D p m	S X p m	p m	Sundays p m	p m
WHITBY TOWN	7.02	7.38	8.48	8.55	9.33	10.22	11.48	12.45	2.00	3.15	5.53	6.56	7.00	7.10
RUSWARP	7.05	7.41	8.53	9.00			11.51	12.48	2.04	3.18		7.01		
SLEIGHTS	7.09	7.45	8.57	9.04			11.55	12.52	2.08	3.22		7.06		7.17
GROSMONT	7.17	7.53	9.06	9.13	9.48	10.36	12.03	1.00	2.17	3.30		7.15		7.26
GOATHLAND	7.26	8.02	9.16	9.23	9.58	10.48	12.12	1.10	2.26	3.39		7.25	7.21	7.37
LEVISHAM	7.41		9.33	9.40		11.05	12.27		2.45	3.54		7.42		7.54
PICKERING	7.53		9.45	9.53	10.26	11.22	12.39		2.58	4.07		7.55	7.52	8.08
MARISHES ROAD	7.59						12.45					8.01		
MALTON	8.10		10.00	10.10	10.43	11.37	12.56		3.13	4.22	7.03	8.15	8.09	8.24
YORK	8.40		10.55*	10.40	11.20	12.07	1.14		3.44	4.51	7.36	8.57*	8.38	8.57

*   Change at Malton   SO   Saturdays Only   SX   Saturdays Excepted   D   Diesel Train

The Esk Valley in later years

A DMU exchanging tokens at Castleton Moor on 2 August 1981. The passing loop, signal box and second platform were all removed the following year.
(G W Morrison)

Research published in *Volume Two* explains the case for retaining only the Middlesbrough route. According to "official figures", it was the least unprofitable of the three lines into Whitby and it carried the greatest year round traffic. Moreover, much of this traffic comprised school children and others from the Esk Valley villages into Whitby. As there is no parallel road, it would have been difficult to provide alternative transport.

In addition, there remained a small volume of freight and there was, at that time, the prospect of traffic from a potash mine between Whitby and Hawsker. There was no immediate prospect of the Esk Valley line being abandoned so, in terms of slowing down Government policy, a reprieve for the Esk Valley passenger service was only a modest frustration.

The reprieve did not affect the closure of most stations to goods traffic. Kildale had closed in 1956, whilst Commondale never had goods facilities. All the other stations continued to handle freight until January 1964, when Battersby lost the facility. Ormesby, and Nunthorpe closed at the same time as Guisborough, in August that year. At the end of July 1965, goods facilities were withdrawn from nearly all the other stations; Great Ayton, Stokesley, Danby, Lealholm, Glaisdale, Egton, Grosmont, Sleights (except for coal) and Ruswarp. The pick up goods continued to serve Castleton, Sleights and Whitby once a week. On other days, if the Station Master

Tom Robertson (a founder of the NYMR) wanted wagons moving, he did it himself using a DMU, which had a layover in the station, whilst the crew took their meal break.

Up to 1965, there had been 46 on the pay roll at Whitby Station. With closure of the two southern routes, this number went down to 18. The biggest change affected drivers and guards because the remaining service was worked from Thornaby. Of the 11 Whitby drivers, four moved to Thornaby but seven took redundancy.

Ruswarp, Sleights and Grosmont also saw a reduction in staff and came under the Whitby Station Master. The incumbent at Sleights, Mr Pratt who also had responsibility for Ruswarp, moved to the booking office at Whitby. So did Ron Cana, the Station Master at Grosmont who also had responsibility for Goathland since the last resident left there in 1963. He remained at Whitby until 1988, also retaining the coal business, which had gone with the position at Grosmont. He was an early member of the NYMR. Another displaced Station Master working in Whitby booking office was Charles Goodall, whom Stuart met in the opening chapter on the last day at Sandsend in 1958.

Clerks, porters and signalmen were made redundant at Ruswarp, Sleights and Grosmont, being replaced by a porter signalman. Another NYMR founder, Charlie Hart, retained his signalman's grade by moving from Ruswarp to Whitby box.

Traditionally, every station had a ticket office and every ticket was collected at the end of the journey, sorted back into numerical order and sent to the audit office. The arrival of a train at even the smallest station, was attended by a porter who opened and shut the doors, collected the tickets and called "when your ready" to the guard who, after satisfying himself that all was well, showed a green flag or lamp to the driver, except on a DMU when he pressed a buzzer.

The guard had little, if any, contact with the passengers. He rode in the guard's van or brake compartment, which was often full of miscellaneous traffic to be loaded and off loaded at stations.

Commondale had become an unstaffed halt in 1950, Kildale followed in 1956 and Great Ayton in 1962. The public timetable warned passengers that there would be "no staff in attendance" at these places. Elsewhere traditional practice continued until 4 May 1969 when the "paytrain" concept was introduced on many routes in the North East.

Staff were withdrawn at all stations between Ormesby and Ruswarp. The guard issued tickets from an Almex machine, which produced the most flimsy tiny slip of paper. Only single tickets were issued. Even passengers joining at Middlesbrough and Whitby were subject to this regime, unless they were travelling beyond the branch. There were no return tickets for local journeys and no through tickets to/ or from intermediate stations. The lines from Middlesbrough to Newcastle, Darlington and Saltburn also became "paytrain" routes. Middlesbrough and Whitby booking offices remained open for enquiries, long distance and season tickets.

It was only during the 1980s that they introduced the more sensible principle that you buy a ticket from the booking office, where there is one, and from the guard when joining at an unstaffed station. From about 1987, the guard could issue a ticket on

his PORTIS machine from and to anywhere, though he might need to consult a fares manual if the request fell outside the limited memory of the machine. Since the mid 2000s, Avantix machines have been in use. These carry all national fares as well as the timetable in their memory.

Whitby still handled parcels and luggage in advance. Two van drivers were amongst the staff retained after 1965. From 1 January 1969, the entire BR delivery fleet of lorries, vans and mechanical horses, was transferred to National Carriers from whom BR continued to contract collection and delivery services at a declining number of stations until the entire function was abolished in 1981. In part compensation, BR developed "Red Star" parcels, a premium station to station service in which Whitby participated until 1988.

Gradually, the double track sections were reduced to single. Grosmont to Sleights was dealt with in 1972. Grosmont box was closed and the section became Glaisdale to Sleights. A ground frame was retained for access to the North Yorkshire Moors Railway.

Castleton closed for goods in June 1982. The signal box and passing loop were eliminated the following month. The pick up goods stopped altogether in May 1983. The track was then singled between Sleights and Whitby in September 1984. Sleights, Bog Hall and Whitby boxes were abolished. Ruswarp survived as a gate box until 1986. At Whitby, only platform No 1 retained any track. Normally, a DMU would just run in and depart again. But they did keep two sidings at Bog Hall, into which a train can retreat. Once it is locked off the main line, the driver can replace the token, allowing another train to approach from Glaisdale.

The Middlesbrough to Nunthorpe section was singled in January 1986. Then, in August 1989, Battersby and Glaisdale boxes were closed. The simplified layout at Battersby is controlled from Nunthorpe box. The driver exchanges key tokens at a small cabin on the one remaining platform. There

Egton retains its main building but not in railway use. A Middlesbrough to Whitby DMU arrives in September 1985. *(David Farrar)*

is no longer any track in the bay, but there is a run round loop through what used to be the Stokesley bound platform. Two DMUs can still pass. One simply goes further along the main platform and the other comes in behind.

At Glaisdale, a white light indicates to approaching trains that the facing point is locked. The train proceeds into the station where the driver exchanges tokens. To save him a walk and loss of time, there are cabins for this purpose on each platform. As time goes on, the machines on the Whitby platform will accumulate Battersby tokens and run out of Whitby ones, with the reverse happening on the other side. Once a week, a Network Rail supervisor has to drive to Glaisdale and, when there is no train in either section, move tokens two at a time from one platform to the other.

Whitby ticket office had booked its last passenger on 10 September 1988 and had ceased handling "Red Star" parcels. After the 1989 signalling changes, there were no staff "on the ground" south of Nunthorpe.

The numbers travelling appeared to be holding up well. In 1975, a 33% increase was recorded. "A striking example of how passengers can be attracted to branch line services by a vigorous all year round publicity effort". (*Modern Railways*) July 1975.

In May 1976, a slightly improved timetable was introduced giving nine trains each way on weekdays and five on Sundays in summer and seven weekdays only in winter. The trains were spaced at roughly two hourly intervals with the summer extras increasing this to hourly towards Whitby in the morning and towards Middlesbrough in the late afternoon.

Between Middlesbrough and Nunthorpe, there had always been a few peak hour short workings, a hang over from the Guisborough line. The service over this part of the route was stepped up in 1976 to give an hourly train throughout most of the day. An additional station was opened at Gypsy Lane. In the morning peak, three trains from Nunthorpe had bus connections from Guisborough, with through tickets marketed under the name "Easyway". The corresponding return trains left Middlesbrough at 17.10, 1740 and 18.10.

By 1988, the Whitby service had eased back to seven trains all year round with four on summer Sundays. The Nunthorpe short workings had also seen a slight reduction whilst the Guisborough buses had gone the way of most attempts at road rail co-ordination.

In October 1990, the number of Whitby trains was reduced to four each way on both weekdays and summer Sundays giving the town its worst rail service since the arrival of the first steam train in 1847. The remaining service was timed around the school traffic. BR claimed that most of the passenger business was being retained by the less frequent service.

This level has prevailed through all the changes of the privatisation era, except that the summer Sunday service has managed to creep up to five trains. By 1998, the Nunthorpe locals were down to two one way and three the other. From December 2007, they have risen again to six each way, in addition to the four Whitby trains.

Twice during 1997, Whitby was visited by the replica of Captain Cook's "Endeavour" which brought extra business to the town. The then recently privatised Regional Railways North East responded with extra trains. On the second occasion, from 12 to 15 December, a preserved class 201 "Hastings" unit was deployed.

The main station buildings at Whitby have been cleaned and transformed into a retail development with one rail track occupying a rather subordinate position. Demolition on the harbour side of the station has exposed to full view the York & North Midland portico, which was previously obscured.

A mainstay of Esk Valley traffic has always been the school children. In 2004, Arriva refurbished the class 144s DMUs, improving the quality of seating but reducing the number of seats. The North

The depth to which Whitby Station had sunk by June 1987. 143 008 departs for Middlesbrough from the one remaining tracked platform. All that remains is to clear the rest of the site for a supermarket. Materials from the signal box will find their way to Grosmont and the former locomen's messroom, the wooden building on the left, will be re erected on the platform at Pickering.
(John Bateman)

Yorkshire Education Authority responded by withdrawing the passes of children travelling from Castleton and Danby to Whitby and organised buses instead. That took away more than a quarter of the 200 or so children travelling by train to school in Whitby.

The problem is the cost of rolling stock. In the 1970s, the "school train" was normally a five coach formation, three for the children and two for other passengers. That was when BR owned the rolling stock. In the post privatisation world, the operating company must lease equipment, which is itself in very short supply, due to the growth of rail travel generally.

In the early 2000s Arriva considered but dismissed the possibility of acquiring the two class 151s for use on the Esk Valley. These were three car DMUs built by Metro Cammell in 1985. They only ran until 1989, mainly around Derby. Teething problems were never resolved. No more were built beyond the two prototypes and they probably died for lack of enthusiasm for their non standard design. For the next 15 years they were shunted around gradually deteriorating until they were scrapped in 2004.

Free bus travel for over 60s must surely pose a threat to the Esk Valley line. The Government is bribing a quarter of the population to go by bus rather than train. It doesn't matter in the PTE areas where there are concessions on trains also. Nor does it matter on lines where the trains are full anyway. For some intermediate journeys in the Esk Valley, there simply are no buses. But for the through journey from Middlesbrough, the bus service is a lot more frequent, faster and free for a significant proportion of the population.

Even if rolling stock became available, a return to the more frequent pre 1990 train service would be impossible. The paths have been allocated to the North Yorkshire Moors Railway. Northern Rail made no objection to this, an indication that they foresee no increase in their own Whitby service.

An early victim of privatisation was the semi steady flow of charter trains to Whitby. During 1993, there were 32 but the following year only two. On 1 April 1994, the infrastructure and signalling were transferred from BR to Railtrack, whose first priority was to organise its business in readiness for the public flotation, which took place in 1996. The allegation was that Railtrack had priced off charter trains.

Most potential charter train paths are now taken up by the NYMR service. The only train operator to object to this was West Coast Railway, the likely operator of any charter trains. The Office of Rail Regulation decreed that actual NYMR operation was of greater benefit than reserving empty paths for speculative and highly infrequent charter trains.

On 11 October 2007, Whitby became a staffed station again with the booking office manned by the NYMR. This is for the sale of all national rail tickets as well as those for the NYMR.

A Journey Through the Esk Valley

Middlesbrough Station dates from 1877. The overall roof was destroyed during the Second World War. The station is well restored with an impressive stone cleaned façade outside and a spacious concourse. The platforms are surmounted by canopies but there is no longer a bay for Whitby trains, which can depart from either of the through platforms.

The Whitby line diverges at Guisborough Junction, where the 140 lever box stood in the angle of the junction. It was destroyed by arson on 7 June 1980. A temporary box was then provided until the junction was placed under Middlesbrough box on 9 May 1982. Only a short distance round the curve is Cargo Fleet Road level crossing. Between 1884 and 1987, this was guarded by a small signal box but is now worked by cctv from Middlesbrough.

Marton Station, formerly Ormesby, is just a bare platform. Here begins the 1 in 44 Nunthorpe Bank, which must have been a problem for ironstone trains, even though they were empty in the uphill direction. It poses no problem for today's class 156 DMU, though one can still sense that the engines are having to work hard. Part way up the Bank is Gypsy Lane Station at Marton Lane level crossing. It had two platforms when opened in 1976 but there is no sign of the other one now.

At Nunthorpe the main station building still bears a number plate B3, a relic from Stockton & Darlington days. Buildings were numbered by branch, the prefix B denoting the Guisborough line.

Leaving Nunthorpe the scenery becomes rural and remains so for the rest of the journey. There is another flashing light level crossing at Morton Carr before we curve sharply to the right at what was Nunthorpe Junction, leaving the disused track bed, now a footpath, towards Guisborough.

To the left, the skyline is dominated by Roseberry Topping, a peak in the Cleveland Hills which rises to 1,051 feet. Great Ayton Station is 1½ miles distant from the picturesque village of that name.

The settlement around Battersby Station is called Battersby Junction. It comprises two parallel streets of terraced houses, originally built for railway staff. There is also a new development called Railway Sidings. The village of Battersby itself is half a mile to the east. The station was called Ingleby Junction until 1878 when it became Battersby Junction. It was abbreviated to Battersby in 1893.

The derelict area to the south of the station was occupied by the engine shed and marshalling sidings. The water tower remains as a memorial. The station building and station master's house have both been restored as private dwellings. In 2005/6, only 839 tickets were issued for travel from Battersby. That is about one ticket for every three trains, the second lowest on the line. Kildale is slightly worse. There is some population within the potential catchment area and there is a free station car park. But the first train to Middlesbrough is not until 9.53am.

A rare visitor to Whitby. Deltic No 55002 "The Kings Own Yorkshire Light Infantry" passing Bog Hall Junction with a return excursion on 2 August 1981. The loco is now preserved at the National Railway Museum, York   *(G W Morrison)*

Virtually the sole purpose of the station is as a reversal point. The train ventures part way along the one remaining platform. Only on the rare occasion when a locomotive needs to run round are the tracks used past the station building and up to the buffer stop which blocks off the route to Picton. Parliamentary powers existed for a north to east curve, which would have avoided Battersby, but it was never built. In 1864 ironstone from Rosedale was far more important than passengers to Whitby.

At the platform end, the 1907 NER water column has been restored to working order for occasional use by locos from the North Yorkshire Moors Railway. When the signal box closed in 1989, there was nobody to feed the fish in the water tank and they died.

At a cabinet on the platform, the driver exchanges the Nunthorpe token for the one to Glaisdale. Then we set off the other way but soon have to slow down for the level crossing at Battersby Road. This is protected by flashing lights. In manual days, it was regulated by a rotating board signal. Kildale Station is much reduced in size. Before 1956, it had two platforms twice the length of the remaining one. The footbridge is not part of the station but carries a path over the railway to the church.

Kildale is on the River Leven which flows through Great Ayton and then meanders to join the Tees near Yarm. Leaving Kildale, the railway follows the Leven closely for about two miles through rather bleak moorland until it reaches the watershed. Then after passing through a cutting, it encounters Sleddale Beck, a tributary of the River Esk, which flows towards Whitby.

The railway runs alongside Sleddale Beck for two miles then crosses it just before Commondale. This is the most remote station on the line, measured by never having had goods facilities and having been the first to become unstaffed in 1950. Traces can be seen of the mile long branch which ran northwards to a brickworks. There are four more bridges over the Beck in the section to Castleton, where it flows into the River Esk. The railway passes through woodlands and then takes a sharp curve into Castleton Moor Station.

The next four stations have buildings with stepped gable ends which are also seen at Goathland and used to feature on other NER branch lines built in the 1860s. Glaisdale remains the only passing point between Battersby and Whitby. The driver must again telephone Nunthorpe box and exchange the Battersby token for a Whitby one.

The stretch of line between Glaisdale and Egton

Grant Rail Matisa Tamping Machine at Whitby on 17 February 2002 during a period of closure for track renewal.
(Martin Bairstow)

is the most picturesque on the entire route. Passing through a wooded gorge, the train crosses the river three times in quick succession. The bridge with the high girders is the one which caused so much trouble in the early 1930s.

There are no fewer than 18 bridges across the Esk between Danby and Ruswarp, nine on either side of Grosmont. There is also one just before Grosmont over the Murk Esk, the tributary which flows in from Beck Hole.

As a reminder of the historical origins of our route, the mileposts since Battersby have given the distance from Picton Junction. Beyond Grosmont, they will be measured from Rillington. It seems barely conceivable that 125 years ago, the area to the north of Grosmont station was occupied by the huge blast furnaces of Grosmont Ironworks. It's also hard to imagine that the angle between platforms 1 and 2, now a car park, was once a goods yard with two camping coaches.

In 1988, the Esk Valley single track was slewed onto the north side of the formation leaving Grosmont to make way for extension of the North Yorkshire Moors platforms and beyond them the carriage sidings.

There were once a number of private sidings between Grosmont and Sleights serving other bygone industries. Today all is rural as the train negotiates the many curves through the lower Esk Valley. The hills close in towards the River alternately on one side then the other forcing the railway to keep re-crossing the Esk. All nine river bridges began life as single track wooden structures in Whitby & Pickering days. They were rebuilt in iron for double track when the York & North Midland upgraded the line for steam.

The girder bridge carrying the main road over the line, just before Sleights station was built in the 1930s to replace a level crossing. The final bridge over the Esk, just before Ruswarp, used to carry a pedestrian right of way on the south side. Ruswarp marks the beginning of the tidal estuary and for the rest of the journey small boats can be seen either

navigating the Esk or marooned in the mud at low tide. The railway takes a sharp curve to the right and Larpool Viaduct comes into view. 120 feet high, with 12 brick arches, our train would be passing over it in about 15 minutes time, were we still permitted to go through to Scarborough. To my regret, I never went over Larpool Viaduct by train though I did do it illicitly on a platelayer's trolley in 1972. At least, since 2000, we can all do it legally on foot or bicycle.

Trains from both Loftus and Scarborough directions used to climb down the embankment on our left, passing under the penultimate arch of the viaduct before reaching our level at Bog Hall Junction. The signal box here survived until 1983 because it controlled access to the goods yard. Two sidings remain, otherwise loco hauled trains could not run round. These are accessed from the Whitby end, where our track simply runs into platform No 1 and stops. The driver inserts the Glaisdale token into the Tyer's machine housed in a cabinet on the platform. Usually, he immediately asks Nunthorpe box for permission to take it back out for the return Journey. The overall roof was removed in 1953. Track was removed from all but platform No 1 in 1984, since when parts of the station, including the bay platforms and goods shed have been sold off to build a supermarket. The end and side porticos still remain, preserving some impression of what had been a G T Andrews station.

Coming out of semi isolation

In most areas, railway passenger traffic is at an all time high and rising. The conditions, which once led to decline, are now having the reverse effect. As car ownership rises, so does rail travel. The motor car creates congestion, at the same time affording easier access to the rail network.

Almost alone amongst towns with a rail service, Whitby is unable to participate in the general trend. From the North East, a journey to Whitby is both slower and less frequent than it was a hundred years ago. From anywhere else it is all but impossible.

The problems are four fold:
(1) Closure of the direct route
(2) Slow Esk Valley line
(3) Low frequency
(4) Poor connections

Item (1) we're lumbered with. Likewise (2). To make any inroad you'd have to eliminate the reversal at Battersby, introduce tokenless block, upgrade level crossings and maybe close the least used stations.

Item (3) is very difficult without equally heavy expenditure. Besides the problem of rolling stock leasing, the NYMR has taken nearly all the spare paths.

Perhaps item (4) offers the best scope for improvement. Between 1982 and 1987, most Whitby trains ran through to and from Darlington. If that facility were restored, Whitby would have connections off East Coast, Cross Country and Trans Pennine at Darlington in addition to Trans Pennine at Middlesbrough.

Even now, with a swift connection at Middlesbrough, the journey from York to Whitby requires only ¾ hour more than it used to take via Malton and Pickering. Given the increase in speed and frequency of trains on the main line, this penalty should not prevent rail travel to Whitby. The further you're travelling, the less significant the detour. From many originating points, the overall journey can be a lot faster than it ever was in the days of the more direct route.

Cross Country don't even show Whitby amongst their connectional services. National Express East Coast advertise connections and through bookings to Whitby by means of a bus from York. There is no reason why a train connection at Darlington should not be just as effective. Many rail travellers might prefer a class 156 from Darlington to a 55 mile bus ride.

Integrated transport
With only four services a day, the train via Darlington or Middlesbrough is never going to give a comprehensive service to Whitby. What is also required is something which was promised, but not delivered, at the time of the 1965 closures. The York – Malton - Whitby and Scarborough – Whitby buses should be offered as a back up to the rail network with maximum flexibility of ticketing. These buses serve the railway stations and are at least as frequent as any train service would be. And yet, I strongly suspect that the number using them to complete longer distance rail journeys is minimal.

In the overwhelming majority of cases, traffic to Whitby is lost to rail throughout because of the difficulty in completing the last leg of the journey. Since 1965, the Railway's response to Whitby has been "its closed" or "you can only get there from Middlesbrough" or "go to Scarborough and get a bus, times for which we cannot supply"

In fact, the Yorkshire Coastliner bus timetable is a lot better than in former times and (Winter 2007/8) some buses do connect with trains at Malton, hourly to Pickering and two hourly to Whitby. The through ticket, now available from any National Rail station, requires the change to be made at York. In many cases, this will extend the journey by an hour, compared to staying with the train to Malton, which is just stupid.

Since the 1998 edition of this book, there has been a little progress but there remains an enormous credibility gap to overcome. The services are running and technology exists to make them available as never before. We need a situation where, on keying Whitby on National Rail enquiries, you would see all the options, train all the way, bus via York, Malton or Scarborough and the fares need to be as interchangeable as they would, were all the options by rail throughout.

The Privatised Railway
A game of musical chairs
On the break up of BR, local trains in the North East, as well as Trans Pennine services, became Regional Railways North East. In February 1997, a seven year franchise was awarded to MTL Trust Holdings Ltd, an employee buy out of Merseyside buses. They kept the cumbersome name Regional Railways North East for the first year, then came up with "Northern Spirit" in 1998.

Never the twain shall meet? Departing Malton for Whitby. SBW30 in 1957, 41251 in 1962.

(J C W Halliday, David Beeken)

The MTL bid had been based on totally unrealistic forecasts of revenue growth and cost reductions. By the end of 1999, the enterprise had collapsed. In February 2000, the franchise was transferred to Arriva, supposedly for two years, after which Trans Pennine and local services were to be separated and both subjected to a new round of bidding. "Northern Spirit" was abandoned in May 2001, in favour of "Arriva Trains Northern".

The re-franchising process got delayed. The Trans Pennine franchise began on 1 February 2004, awarded to First Group for eight years. Arriva continued to run local trains until the Northern Rail franchise began on 12 December 2004. This combines services in the North West and runs for eight years and nine months.

In preparation for privatisation, the BR parcels sector was renamed Rail Express Systems whilst the freight sector was divided into three companies, Trans-Rail, Mainline and Load-Haul to encourage competition. The whole lot were sold to Wisconsin Central in 1995/6 and became English Welsh & Scottish Railway. Freightliner was privatised separately.

Intercity East Coast became Great North Eastern Railway in April 1996, with a seven year franchise, later extended by two years and eventually renewed for a further ten years in 2005. The renewal bid was unrealistic. The collapse of the parent company, Sea Containers, led to termination of the franchise, which was awarded to National Express East Coast for seven years and three months from December 2007.

The Intercity Cross Country franchise was awarded to Virgin Group for 15 years from January 1997. The bid proved too optimistic and was terminated early. A new franchise of eight years and four months began on 11 November 2007, bringing Arriva back onto the scene. Their first visible act has been to remove the names from the class 220 and class 221 trains.

The franchise terms are so short that they scarcely get the fleets repainted before its time to change again.

Since 2005, class 156 units have been the regular power on the Esk Valley service. 156 468 calls at Sleights, bound for Middlesbrough.   *(Neil Buxton)*

Cleveland Potash

In the late 1960s, two planning applications were made to sink potash mines on the coast of North Yorkshire. In both cases it was promised that output would be moved by rail both on environmental grounds and for sheer practical reasons that this was the best way of transporting it.

One site was at Stainsacre just to the north of Hawsker. Until 1973, track was left in situ along the disused line from Bog Hall Junction via Prospect Hill over Larpool viaduct and as far as Hawsker Station. Unfortunately planning objections and a fall in the price of potash combined to kill the project which would have guaranteed a heavy freight traffic the length of the Esk Valley besides bringing back to life the northern most part of the Scarborough line.

Further north at Boulby the story is very different. Here Cleveland Potash despatches up to eight train loads per day. Following closure of the passenger service to Loftus in 1960, the railway had been cut back to Skinningrove which continued to be served via Saltburn Junction. The decision to go ahead with Boulby mine led to the rebuilding of four miles of railway through Loftus and Grinkle to a point about one mile short of Staithes. Various bridges which had been demolished were reinstated and the line came back to use in April 1974.

Potash is carried in 93 tonne bogie hoppers either to Tees Dock for export, to Middlesbrough for onward transport by road or direct by rail to Ely and Severnside. In addition rock salt is mined at Boulby and carried out by rail for sale to local authorities for de-icing roads.

Ventures by passenger trains onto the restored line have been very few. A Branch Line Society railtour on 22 March 1986 was the first public excursion to reach Boulby.

20119 and 20165 in charge of a potash train from Boulby passing Skinningrove on 30 March 1989. At privatisation, the operation passed to English Welsh & Scottish Railway but in April 2007 the contract was won by Freightliner who employ their class 66/6 locos.

(John Bateman)

Crag Hall, between Brotton and Skinningrove, marked the end of the double track. The signalman is ready with the token for Loftus. The box closed In February 1970 when the line from Saltburn was singled. It reopened on 1 April 1974 with tokenless block from Saltburn and electric token to Boulby.

(David R Smith)

37079 heads a loaded potash train round the curve from Brotton towards North Skelton on 20 September 1982.
(Tom Heavyside)

The first public passenger train to reach Boulby, the Branch Line Society tour of 22 March 1986.
(David Farrar)

Passengers to Loftus?

Since the 1980s a number of closed lines have had their passenger trains restored. In most cases the routes had retained, or only recently lost, their freight traffic so the tracks had never been lifted.

There is no shortage of studies being carried out into the possibility of further reopenings, in some cases of lines which have been completely abandoned and sold off.

Against this background it seems odd that there has been no suggestion of restoring passenger trains between Saltburn and Loftus.

The combined populations of Skelton, Brotton and Loftus exceed 20,000. There is a half hourly service as far as Saltburn (population 9,000). It would be possible to extend one train per hour as far as Loftus at the cost of one additional dmu. An extra passing loop would be required at Brotton in addition to the one at Crag Hall in order to retain the freight capacity.

The train would hardly be fast between Loftus and Saltburn. The distance by rail is nine miles including reversal at Saltburn West, double that by road. But the train would be through to Middlesbrough and Darlington.

Whether the idea is feasible depends on how far the pendulum swings back in favour of rail. Compared with some candidates for reopening, this route has the distinct advantage that it does not require to be reauthorised, repurchased and rebuilt. With its gradients, curves and cliff top views, it would certainly be an interesting journey.

MIDDLESBROUGH–LOFTUS

5th May to 7th June, 1958

	Weekdays							
	a.m.	a.m.	a.m.	S.X. p.m.	S.O. p.m.	p.m.	p.m.	p.m.
Middlesbrough... dep.	6 45	9 15	11 15	12 27	12 27	2 27	5 35	8 0
Ormesby	6 51	9 21	11 21	12 33	12 33	2 33	5 41	8 6
Nunthorpe	6 57	9 27	11 27	12 39	12 39	2 39	5 47	8 12
Hutton Gate	7 4	9 34	11 34	12 46	12 46	2 46	5 54	8 19
Guisborough	7 10	9 38	11 38	12 50	12 50	2 50	5 58	8 23
Boosbeck	7 19	9 47	...	...	12 59	2 59	6 7	...
Brotton	7 27	9 54	...	...	1 6	3 6	6 14	...
Loftus ... ... arr.	7 36	10 3	...	...	1 15	3 15	6 23	...

LOFTUS–MIDDLESBROUGH

	Weekdays							
	a.m.	a.m.	a.m.	S.X. p.m.	S.O. p.m.	p.m.	p.m.	p.m.
Loftus ... ... dep.	7 46	10 18	...	...	1 30	3 30	7 0	...
Brotton	7 57	10 29	...	...	1 41	3 41	7 11	...
Boosbeck	8 4	10 36	...	...	1 48	3 48	7 18	...
Guisborough	8 12	10 44	11 45	1 33	1 56	3 56	7 26	9 16
Hutton Gate	8 16	10 48	11 49	1 37	2 0	4 0	7 30	9 20
Nunthorpe	8 22	10 54	11 55	1 43	2 6	4 6	7 36	9 26
Ormesby	8 26	10 58	11 59	1 47	2 10	4 10	7 40	9 30
Middlesbrough... arr.	8 32	11 4	12 5 p.m.	1 53	2 16	4 16	7 46	9 36

S.O.—Saturdays only.   **S.X.**—Saturdays excepted.

For two years after closure of the coast line, Loftus retained a dmu service to Middlesbrough.

Loftus Station photographed from a northbound train on a wet 26 April 1958. The buildings have gone but the goods yard is empty – waiting to serve as a park & ride facility?   *(J C W Halliday)*

The North Yorkshire Moors Railway

Deltic No 55009 "Alycidon" passing Grosmont engine shed on 9 June 1985. Sold by BR in 1982, it came immediately to the NYMR. In 1990, it was withdrawn for a major overhaul and is now in working order at the Deltic Preservation Society site at Barrow Hill. *(G W Morrison)*

If there were any lingering hopes that the events of 6 March 1965 were other than final, these quickly evaporated. Talk of the Malton to Whitby service being taken over by a private company and/or being subsidised by local councils was at least 20 years ahead of its time. A train did in fact run from Whitby to Goathland in November 1965 when all roads to the village were blocked by snow. Whilst this may have confirmed the value of the railway to those who had opposed closure, it did not bring about the hoped for re-examination of the case and that dmu proved to be the last train over the line operated by British Railways.

By the Summer of 1967, it looked as though track lifting was about to commence but on 3 June a small meeting was held at the home of one of the founders of what was to become the North Yorkshire Moors Railway. At a public meeting at Goathland in October, the NYMR Preservation Society was formed with the object of acquiring at least a part of the Grosmont to Pickering line with a view to operating it primarily as a tourist facility with volunteer staff.

British Railways gave the Society six months to produce a viable scheme during which time track lifting was postponed. In 1968 it was agreed that the Society would buy the line from Grosmont to Goathland Summit signal box together with the land

from that point to Pickering. It was envisaged that a terminus to be known as Ellerbeck would be established at the Summit where the Lyke Wake Walk goes across the railway and this would be the limit of the new railway unless and until it were to prove so successful as to allow progressive rebuilding towards Pickering.

At that stage it was believed that acquisition of the track between Ellerbeck and Pickering would be beyond the resources of the Society. In addition it was considered that the proposed 6½ mile railway marked the limit of what could be handled by a voluntary society. In the Autumn of 1968, BR gave the Preservation Society permission to work on the line and so began the long haul towards reopening. On 2 February 1969, the first train movement took place when 'Mirvale', a Hudswell Clarke 0-4-0 saddle tank, was steamed at Pickering and driven through to Grosmont where the tunnel provided under cover accommodation for the Society's first rolling stock acquisitions.

Society members were able to travel between Grosmont and Goathland on three 'open weekends' during the Summer of 1970 but it was still three years before the railway could reopen to the public. It had been intended that the process of transferring ownership of the railway would follow the pattern established by the Keighley & Worth Valley Railway which had reopened in 1968. This would involve the formation of an operating company in which the Preservation Society would have a substantial holding.

British Railways would then apply for a light railway order bringing the line within the jurisdiction of the Light Railways Act 1896 followed by a Transfer Order conferring operating powers on the NYMR Company. The use of the light railway order was at that time the only way to transfer ownership of a railway without special legislation.

On 27 March 1971, the functions of both the NYMR Preservation Society and its recently formed operating company were transferred to the North Yorkshire Moors Historical Railway Trust. This body, which is controlled by its membership, has charitable status with resultant tax exemptions including the opportunity for members to covenant subscriptions and donations. The 'Historical' in the title drew attention to the educational part of the Trust's objects. Previously charitable status had been refused to organisations which put railway operation as their main objective. In addition, the Trust was emphasising the historical significance of the Whitby & Pickering Railway in negotiations with the North Riding County Council, its National Park Committee and the English Tourist Board.

These bodies agreed financial support for the NYMR provided that it operated the full 18 miles from Grosmont to Pickering. The County Council purchased the track south of the Summit and leased it to the railway.

The proposed terminus at Ellerbeck never happened. When the NYMR opened to the public on 22 April 1973, it was at 18 miles the longest preserved railway in the Country. There were many, including quite a few people within the NYMR itself, who argued that the Trust had taken on more than it could handle. The scale of the operation, together with its remoteness from the centres of population meant that it could not rely solely on volunteer labour. With a sizeable wages bill, the NYMR cannot hope to plough back into the business the same proportion of its income as can be achieved with an all voluntary operation. The railway started off undercapitalised and it was a very slow process for this deficiency to be made good. Inevitably there were some disasters on the way.

In the first summer (the NYMR has so far only operated on a seasonal basis), there were steam trains between Grosmont and Goathland augmented on Saturdays and Sundays only by a dmu running all the way to Pickering. Strictly these trains ran to a point just short of Pickering because of a dispute between the railway, which was backed by the County Council, and the local Council which wanted to see the station demolished and the site redeveloped. Until this was resolved, trains terminated at a temporary platform just north of High Mill level crossing.

1974 saw trains running to Pickering on weekdays during the Summer season but still restricted to the two twin car dmu sets. From 24 May 1975 they were at last able to run into Pickering Station itself.

By way of apologising for the use of diesel power, which at that time had yet to find much support on preserved railways, the NYMR blamed the risk of fire in Newtondale for the decision not to run steam south of Goathland. The truth was that they did not have the steam power with which to do it at the time. 1976 promised a start to regular steam services to Pickering but the extraordinary hot and dry summer produced a very real fire risk and steam locomotives were banned from the southern section of the line. Since the four dmu cars lacked the capacity for the traffic on offer nor did they have 100% reliability, chaos ensued with some trains being worked at very low speed by a class 08 shunter hired from BR.

The crisis was resolved at the end of the season with the arrival in working order of class 24 No. D5032. This at last gave the NYMR the capability of carrying the numbers of travellers who wished to enjoy the rail journey through Newtondale. It also marked the beginning of a period during which the NYMR became the leader in the field of diesel locomotive preservation. The class 24 was subsequently joined by other BR types including, but not all at the same time, a 31, a Western, Warship and Hymeck, two Deltics and more recently two class 25s.

Built in 1949, K1 No 62005, worked the "Whitby Moors Railtour" on 6 March 1965. Withdrawn in 1967, it was preserved for use on the NYMR where it is seen climbing towards Goathland on 29 April 1984.

(G W Morrison)

The diesels gave the NYMR a much needed break. At last there was sufficient power to move long trains the whole way between Grosmont and Pickering. Gradually through the 1980s, an adequate fleet of steam locomotives was built up allowing a virtual all steam operation. By 1986, rostered diesel power was found only on the first train out of Pickering and the last one back. From 1989, they began to cover even those workings by a steam loco working light engine from and to Grosmont.

Neither Grosmont nor Pickering Stations had been designed for eight coach trains, nor for the volume of passengers who arrived on them. Platforms have had to be lengthened and customer facilities improved. The whole railway has had to become a self contained unit with its own motive power depot and workshops at Grosmont.

The NYMR functions with a mix of paid staff and volunteers. It operates daily from Easter until the end of October with some limited winter services.

On 9 and 10 August 1999, the NYMR made its first venture into the commercial freight market. A scrap yard near Pickering was closing down and English Welsh & Scottish Railway got the contract to move some wagonloads of compressed motor cars to a processing plant on Merseyside. On the first day, EWS No 66024 made its way to New Bridge with the empties, let NYMR 08556 do the shunting, then took away the loaded wagons. The following

day it was 66055. Railtrack said they viewed the operation as an experiment and would want an intermediate token machine at Grosmont before agreeing to regular freight. The machine was installed in 2007 for the Whitby passenger service but no more freight has yet offered.

Steaming back to Whitby
The story of the NYMR has been one of tremendous achievement. Yet the 18 mile railway doesn't really go anywhere. It runs from a sizeable town, with no rail connection, to a small village with a very poor onward service. This "disadvantage" has not prevented the NYMR from carrying more passengers than any other heritage railway.

Pickering is a tourist destination, capable of generating traffic for the Railway and of providing facilities for passengers arriving there by train. The problem is at the northern end of the line. As the editor of *Moors Line* (Winter 1987/88) so aptly put it, many passengers cannot even pronounce the name of the station where they are "dumped" 6½ miles short of the logical destination, which would be Whitby.

The desire of the NYMR to reach Whitby is both emotional and economic. Whitby is at the heart of the rail network, which the NYMR seeks to preserve. Some of the 11 Founders were Whitby railway staff. Even the title of this book is *Railways Around Whitby*, not Grosmont.

Black Five 45407 "The Lancashire Fusilier" leaving Whitby for Glaisdale on 29 May 2006. The sidings in the foreground are used for loco run round. *(Martin Bairstow)*

45407 "The Lancashire Fusilier" has arrived at Whitby from Grosmont on 29 May 2006. *(Martin Bairstow)*

Whitby is full of tourists, a few of whom were being enticed to drive to Grosmont and take a trip on the NYMR, see where *Heartbeat* is filmed and so on. But no amount of publicity in Whitby Tourist Information Centre could rival the message from a steam locomotive hissing and whistling in the town itself.

There is a train service, of sorts, between Whitby and Grosmont. Since 1973, there has been nothing to prevent a family staying in Whitby from taking the full Whitby & Pickering Railway experience. Periodically, there have been through tickets offered for the very purpose. Some people have done it, but not in sufficient numbers to amount to anything.

Up to September 1988, there was a booking office at Whitby, which would have supplied the requisite information, especially when the incumbent was the former Grosmont and Goathland Station Master and a NYMR member. After Whitby lost its staff, it would have been much harder for anyone, other than a seasoned rail traveller, to work out the connection between Whitby Station and the NYMR. With the reduction to four trains a day in 1990, the task will have become harder still.

Even when there were seven trains a day on the Esk Valley, they just didn't connect with the NYMR. Some potential connections were missed by the odd minute. I've never suggested that this was bloody mindedness by either party. That would credit them with having considered the issue. The truth is that both planned their timetables independently without regard to the other's existence. What had a tourist attraction got to do with providing a "lifeline" service to the Esk Valley villages or vice versa?

In Summer 1988, when there were still seven or eight trains each way in the Esk Valley, the NYMR advertised Whitby connections using a mini bus to negotiate the steep and narrow roads out of Grosmont.

From at least the mid 1980s, the NYMR looked to running its own trains into Whitby both to tap the Whitby market and to avoid "dumping" passengers at Grosmont with little or nothing to do there. On Sunday 11 October 1987, No 92220 "Evening Star" worked a service from Pickering to Whitby and back, with two intermediate return trips between Whitby and Goathland. Payments to BR were ten times those for the only similar venture when 62005 had worked through in 1975. Despite this, the event was deemed a qualified success which might be repeated once a year. That proved impossible.

Meanwhile, the local authorities offered assistance in the form of a feasibility study. This proved a complete waste of money, telling us what we already knew. It would be prohibitively expensive to relay the second track between Grosmont and Whitby because the single line had been slewed all over the formation, at least on the stretch, which was singled first, west of Sleights. It would be even more expensive to share the single line with BR as they would insist on all trains being manned by their crews who would have to come from Thornaby and who could not be made available on a seasonal basis.

Not that the NYMR membership was unanimous in wanting to press on to Whitby. Arguments for and against seemed vaguely reminiscent of the previous Ellerbeck – Pickering dilemma. The topic continued to be aired from time to time in *Moors Line*. In the Autumn 1993 issue, Murray Brown argued that rail privatisation might provide the opening. From 1 April 1994, the BR network would pass to Railtrack and would be available, at least in theory, to both franchised operators and other entrepreneurs.

On 22 November 1998, 65894 hauled the Captain Cook Pullman at 12.20 from Pickering to Whitby. This was a premium dining train, operated by Northern Spirit between Grosmont and Whitby. The event was repeated during 1999 but not afterwards.

The breakthrough came in 2003, with trains advertised to run to and from Whitby on the May Day Bank Holiday weekend and again on Spring Bank Holiday Monday and Tuesday. The operator was the West Coast Railway Company, which has a license to run anywhere on Network Rail and which has used NYMR engines on its Fort William to Mallaig service. With a West Coast crew and a token fetched by road from Glaisdale, a NYMR steam train left Grosmont platform 2 for Whitby, whence it provided three departures. The first two ran to Glaisdale with connections for Pickering. The last one ran to Grosmont only, where it came back onto the NYMR and the token was returned by road to Glaisdale.

Further ventures were planned for later in the season until Network Rail announced that the line through Ruswarp was closed to loco hauled trains until such time that the track was relaid.

The offending track was replaced during 2004 and the West Coast operation resumed in 2005 on 22 operating days. With Northern Rail connections also shown in the timetable, a total of six or seven connectional opportunities were available at Grosmont between Whitby and the NYMR. On Whitby running days, NYMR operating hours were extended with a DMU at 8.45am from Pickering to connect with the first steam departure from Grosmont and a corresponding 6.05pm from Grosmont connecting out of the 5.40pm from Whitby. For 2006, the number of Whitby days increased to 50.

Meanwhile, the NYMR had held a postal vote amongst the entire membership seeking approval to become, if it could, a licensed operating company on Network Rail. The result was heavily in favour.

The main physical, as opposed to bureaucratic, requirement was an intermediate token machine at Grosmont. This was commissioned on 4 March 2007, by which time the operating licence had been issued. History was finally made on Tuesday 3 April 2007 when No 62005 took the inaugural press train through from Pickering to Whitby, the first preserved or heritage railway to operate in its own right over the national system. This is also the first instance of volunteer crews working over Network Rail. As on the NYMR proper, either full time or volunteer crews can be rostered, as long as they've been properly trained and examined.

Whitby trains operated on more than 90 days in 2007. Again, there were three departures from Whitby. They no longer ran to Glaisdale but at least as far Goathland. It is planned to run from Whitby on 170 days in 2008, with all trains going through to Pickering. The only peak days with no trains to Whitby are Summer Sundays, when most of the paths are taken by the more frequent Northern trains.

The NYMR has operating rights as far as Battersby. All crews passed for Whitby must also "sign" for the route between Grosmont and Battersby. If a train from Whitby arrived at the junction with the NYMR and the ground frame refused to budge, the driver would have to stop in platform 1, then take the train on to Glaisdale to avoid delaying Northern Rail. Possibly as a means of keeping up route knowledge, the NYMR advertised a Saturday evening steam excursion from Whitby to Battersby during mid Summer 2007.

The arrival of steam trains in Whitby has increased the number of passengers making use of Northern Rail connections at Grosmont. People who would never have sought out a connection from an unstaffed station are finding themselves drawn by the steam service into using the Northern Rail DMU for perhaps one leg of a return journey.

I travelled from Pickering in June 2007, on a Whitby operating day but at times requiring a change at Grosmont in both directions. I've done it before, sometimes the sole occupant of a busy NYMR train who has found his way to platform 1, whilst all the others seemed to believe that they'd reached the end of the line. In 2007, the atmosphere was different. The NYMR station man was directing Whitby people to platform 1. When the Northern Rail DMU came in, he was on platform 1, announcing the train as though he owned it. When the Northern Rail conductor appeared, a number of passengers showed NYMR tickets.

NYMR fares are at a premium compared with Northern Rail so full inter availability is not possible. NYMR tickets are valid on Northern trains. The other way round, an upgrade is required.

On 11 October 2007, the NYMR presence at Whitby was consolidated further when it took charge of the ticket office and car park on behalf of Northern Rail. Whitby became a staffed station for the first time since 1988.

An Opportunity Missed

Long before there was serious hope of reaching Whitby, the NYMR let pass an opportunity to purchase the engine shed, last used for railway purposes in 1959. Instead the building was acquired by the Captain James Cook RN (Charity Trust) Ltd. Their aim is to turn it into a museum and visitor centre, financed in part by residential development on the rest of the site. There has been a lot of opposition to this, including from the NYMR which doesn't like the idea of the station concourse and operational platform becoming the pedestrian access to the museum.

Despite objections, planning permission was granted in November 2007. The Railway may have to adopt the alternative strategy of welcoming a tourist development on its doorstep.

One fear is that it could limit scope for extending platform 1. The NYMR would like a loco run round within the station, to save propelling out to Bog Hall. There is space for a track but the turnout and headshunt would eat into the operational platform length. In order still to accommodate seven coaches, the platform would need extending towards

Grosmont, which Captain Cook may have made more difficult.

There may be some space to be gained at the buffer stop end, if Network Rail would relax their "group standard" for terminal stations. This requires that the track should end short of the original buffer stops, lest a train should overrun and mount the station concourse. At Whitby, arriving steam trains and DMUs would continue to stop some way short of the buffers. Only the run round move would take the loco to the very end.

The Final Frontier?

Assuming that the Whitby venture remains a success and that the NYMR consolidates its position as a 24 mile line, somebody is going to notice a glaring gap in the modern railway map. Actually, they already have. For more than ten years there has been a campaign to reopen from Pickering south to Rillington Junction. Both North Yorkshire and Ryedale Councils have responded with a feasibility study and are pledged to keep the route free of further intrusive development. Matters came to a head in 2001 when there was a planning application for a supermarket, which would have blocked the route between Hungate and Mill Lane in Pickering. It was turned down in part because it would prejudice eventual reopening of the Railway. The councils say that their influence over rail issues is very limited and all they can do is try to stop options being closed before Central Government finally decides to tackle the transport crisis.

As with Pickering and Whitby, there are doubters within the NYMR. I wonder how many of them now would retreat to just Grosmont – Ellerbeck?

Not that they need worry for some time. But if economic growth continues, population rises, more houses are built, car ownership mushrooms further, then transport issues will have to be addressed. Nobody would do today, what was done in March 1965. One day, some of these historic mistakes will have to be put right.

There must be a parallel with the railway map of North Wales, once the Welsh Highland is completed. Perhaps Bangor to Caernarfon is Welsh for Malton to Pickering. At the 2005 AGM of the Welsh Highland Railway Society, a member asked about the prospects for restoring Bangor to Caernarfon. The Chairman responded that the link was inevitable but would have to wait for a future generation.

Perhaps Henry Belcher's prophecy of 1836 will be fulfilled a second time.

There is every prospect of the line being extended from Pickering in the direction of Malton and York, so as to connect the port of Whitby with the central parts of the country and afford to the country generally, and more especially to the inhabitants of the West Riding, an interesting and ready approach to the most romantic part of the Yorkshire Coast.
From *The Scenery of the Whitby & Pickering Railway* (1836)

Metro Cammell (class 101) DMU at Goathland on 29 May 2006. Power cars 51511 and 50204 have since acquired a centre trailer car.
(Martin Bairstow)

A journey on the NYMR

Whitby Station occupies a prominent position in the town centre near the harbour. Most passengers will approach by the G T Andrews portico on the south side. The NYMR office and shop is just to the right of the arches. This sells National Rail as well as NYMR tickets. Despite severe rationalisation in 1984, platform 1 can still accommodate a locomotive and seven coaches. For the engine to run round, the train has to propel out towards Bog Hall. The only signalling is a stop board at the end of the platform which reads "obtain token and permission to proceed". The driver will telephone Nunthorpe box and withdraw the token for Glaisdale, even though he's not going that far.

NYMR trains are not scheduled to stop at Ruswarp but the level crossing is timed for a stopping train. Nor are they booked to stop at Sleights but Whitby bound, they have to stop whilst the driver uses a lineside telephone.

Approaching Grosmont, the single track assumes a position on the northern side of the formation in order to accommodate the NYMR carriage sidings. One day, it is hoped to erect a roof over these, otherwise the carriages are going to deteriorate. The train stops for the fireman to insert the token into the ground frame and pull over the points leading onto the NYMR. The train proceeds into platform 2. The points are reset and the Whitby to Glaisdale token is placed in the Tyer's machine.

The main part of Grosmont Station was built in 1847. The Esk Valley platform 1 was an 1865 addition. There were two platforms on the "main line" to Pickering with a loop round the back of platform 3. In the early 1990s, platform 2 was extended towards Whitby whilst platform 3 was turned into an island with platform 4 facing onto the previous loop. Platforms 3 and 4 were extended in 2004. Some of the materials for this were given by

contractors working on the Sleights to Whitby relaying in return for siding space to stable their plant.

The expansion of Grosmont has involved the re-use of materials from other stations. The platform extensions include coping stones from Helmsley and from the bay platforms at Whitby. Lamp posts and flower tubs were acquired from stations on the Hull to Scarborough line. Most prominent are the clock from Northallerton and the 1913 waiting room from Sleights.

The 1847 Station House, at the Pickering end of Platform 2, has been converted into holiday accommodation. Opposite, the signal box is a NYMR creation of the mid 1990s, built to a design of the 1870s, using bricks recovered from Whitby box. The 52 lever frame is from Horden in County Durham. The signalman has two wheels for opening the level crossing gates. One is for the main gates spanning the platform 2 and 3 lines, the other for the loop, now the platform 4 line. From about 1876 until 1972, Grosmont signal box stood in the angle between the Pickering and Esk Valley lines. The level crossing was opened by hand but controlled from a small lean-to shed, which the NYMR used as a signal box until the present box was commissioned.

The Station Tavern, to the south of the level crossing, is the Tunnel Inn of 1835 which served both as a hostelry and as the Whitby & Pickering station. Set back, between the signal box and the Tavern is a former Post Office and warehouse, also dating from 1835. This was restored by the NYMR in 2000 for use as volunteer accommodation upstairs and as a workshop downstairs. There is evidence that a track once ran into the building. This must have been via a turntable off what is now the platform 4 line.

Leaving Grosmont, the line crosses the Murk Esk by a stone bridge then enters the 120 yard tunnel.

The area south of Grosmont Tunnel has been developed into the NYMR engine shed and workshops. J27 No 2392 (65894), Lambton Colliery 0 – 6- 2T No 29, K1 No 62005 and Black Five No 45428.

(J R P Hunt)

This dates from 1847 when the railway was adapted for locomotive working. The adjacent footpath crosses the river on a bridge, which replaced the timber trestle of the Whitby & Pickering Railway then passes through the much narrower profile tunnel which was used by the horse trains. The path gives access to the NYMR engine sheds and workshops, then crosses the railway to reach the track bed of the Beckhole branch. The whole of the pre 1865 route, including the incline, is a public footpath. Some visitors take the train one way and walk the "Rail Trail" in the other direction.

Beyond the engine shed, at the former Deviation Junction, the train begins to attack the 1 in 49 ascent. For many, this is the highlight of the journey, feeling and hearing the locomotive working hard. At the approach to Goathland there is a sand drag protecting the exit from the passing loop. The gradient eases through the station, which retains the appearance and atmosphere of a country station – except that it is a lot busier. The building with stepped gable ends is in full railway use. The site does not permit extension to the platforms, which are too short for many of the trains. A camping coach occupies the same site as used in LNER and BR days. There are two staff accommodation coaches in the same livery. The biggest structural change is the NER footbridge. In former times it was not thought necessary to provide a footbridge at a quiet place like this but the crowds who now throng the platforms have made it a different matter.

Leaving Goathland, the climb is resumed at a more modest 1 in 90/100. Just before the summit, we can again see the formation of the pre 1865 route as it merges into the present line. Goathland Summit is nearly 550 feet above sea level and stands on top of Fen Bog. This rather soggy relic of the Ice Age was some 20 feet deep at the time the Whitby & Pickering was under construction.

Whole trees covered in moss and heather bound in sheep skins were amongst materials sunk into Fen Bog to produce what turned out to be a very durable foundation. The line begins a series of twists and turns through the bracken and heather which provide much colour to the surrounding moorlands as the train enters Newtondale.

There is no road access to the woodlands on the edge of Pickering Forest only footpaths. In 1981 the NYMR opened Newtondale Halt using materials recovered from Warrenby Halt on the Middlesbrough to Saltburn line, closed when that route was diverted in 1978. A shelter was provided at Newtondale in 2003.

Levisham Station is a remote spot, accessed by a steep minor road from the village, which is 1½ miles to the east and 300 feet higher up. The station and signal box are usually manned but can be left unattended when "long section" staff and ticket working is in use. A switch from "short" to "long" section working entails inserting both the Goathland to Levisham and Levisham to New Bridge staffs at Levisham in order to release the "long section" Goathland to New Bridge staff. Levisham signals are then cleared for trains to run in both directions through the northbound platform. The reverse procedure is required when the section needs to be split again.

Between Levisham and Pickering the line runs through extensive woodlands. Two miles of virtually straight track lead to Farworth, where trains occasionally stop to serve occupants of some former railway cottages. The line again begins to twist and curve as it negotiates the final length of Newtondale. Then the scenery opens out as the train enters the Vale of Pickering.

Grosmont Station House, seen in 1957, now serves as holiday accommodation. The wooden building by the signal was for the crossing keeper. From 1973 until 1996, it served as the NYMR signal box.
(J C W Halliday)

50204/ 51511 on the 8.45am to Grosmont, under the former Walker Gate footbridge at Pickering on 29 May 2006. It is unusual for trains to leave from platform 2.

(Martin Bairstow)

Just before New Bridge, the permanent way department has taken over the former quarry sidings, which provided the last freight traffic up to 1966. The shed was completed in 1998. A servicing facility was opened here in April 2006 so that a steam loco can be kept overnight. Previously, the loco of the last train into Pickering had to return light engine to Grosmont, with a corresponding movement the following morning, necessitating longer signal box hours.

New Bridge box guards a skew level crossing. It is the only survivor amongst the many boxes, which used to control traffic through Pickering with its numerous level crossings. Today, New Bridge works the colour light signals and power operated points in the Pickering Station area.

The final approach to Pickering passes alongside a trout farm. High Mill level crossing, which mainly gives access to the NYMR car park, is protected by flashing lights. The train passes the foot of Pickering Castle and enters the curved platforms. The arrival (former southbound) platform has been extended back towards High Mill. The former locomen's messroom from Whitby has been re-erected on the extension, as has the Gilling porters room, photographed on the title page of *Railways of Ryedale*. The NYMR carriage works have been established opposite the extended platform.

Prior to 1952, Pickering boasted a York & North Midland Railway G T Andrews overall roof, hence the high supporting walls. The main (formerly York bound) platform retains the canopy, which was installed to replace the roof. Although the platform is low in relation to the train, the adjoining rooms used to be even lower, requiring customers to step down into the shop and buffet. This anomaly was rectified as part of the refurbishment about 2000. The locomotive draws forward into a head shunt occupying the short distance to what was Bridge Street level crossing where the line has been walled off.

Footbridges

At wayside stations, the traditional method of getting from one platform to the other was by a sleeper crossing. The numbers using NYMR stations is somewhat greater than in former times, leading to the installation of footbridges at Goathland, Pickering and Grosmont. The Railway was able to obtain authentic North Eastern structures displaced at Howden on Tyne and Walker Gate when the line through those stations was electrified as part of the Tyne & Wear Metro. The former was installed at Goathland in 1986. It is not suitable for the disabled but the old crossing still remains. It has a right of way over it.

The Walker Gate structure was opened at Pickering on 7 April 1997. Since nearly all trains leave from the platform nearest the station buildings and town centre, the main function of the footbridge is to shorten the walk to the car park, accessed from the north end of the far platform. The option remains of taking the longer but level route round the buffer stops.

The footbridge at Grosmont was commissioned in 2001, linking platforms 1 and 2 with the National Park car park on the site of the old iron works. It spans the Esk Valley track and was required to conform to Railtrack (now Network Rail) standards with sufficient clearance for 25,000 volt electrification. The bridge is ex London, Brighton & South Coast Railway. It cost the NYMR very little as it was a County Council project to make better use of the car park and cut down on traffic in the village. About the same time, access was improved between platforms 1 and 2. The whole of Grosmont station has level access from the main entrance by the level crossing.

Rights of Way

When railways were closed, they weren't just left to grow weeds and wait the day when they might be needed again. The closure policy of the 1960s went much farther than that. The tracks and all lineside equipment were removed, usually for scrap, occasionally for use elsewhere. Bridges were removed and, wherever possible, the land was sold off piecemeal.

It was naturally more difficult to find buyers in some of the remoter areas. As much by accident as by intent, some stretches of track bed have survived as footpaths and cycle ways. Only in more recent times has there been any concerted effort to develop dismantled railways for recreational use. This has come after many rights of way had already been destroyed.

One can cycle virtually the whole of the Scarbrough to Whitby line from Gallows Close, near Falsgrave Tunnel, to Prospect Hill Junction. The short missing bits at Scalby and Ravenscar are easily bypassed.

Further north, a 2½ mile stretch of the Guisborough branch is available to walkers and cyclists from Nunthorpe Junction to a point east of Pinchinthorpe where the trail goes off into Guisborough Forest. There is no access at Nunthorpe Junction, only at Pinchinthorpe where both the original Stockton & Darlington and the 1877 North Eastern station houses survive on either side of the road bridge which replaced the level crossing as part of the 1877 alterations.

You can walk, but not cycle, from Goathland to Grosmont, down the incline and along the Beck Hole branch. You can hear the trains battling up the nearby 1 in 49 of the 1865 Deviation, which made the incline redundant.

Another former rope worked incline, now available on foot or bicycle, is that on the Rosedale branch. This closed in 1929 but passes through such wild and remote territory that the track bed has never been redeveloped. Spectacular views can be enjoyed on a clear day. From Blakey Junction, you can observe the long sweep of the East Rosedale branch as it curves round the head of the valley towards its terminus, which is now a farmyard above Hill Cottages.

The track bed can also be walked from Sandsend Station towards Kettleness Tunnel affording a taste of what it was like travelling this scenic coastal line.

Tackling the 1 in 41 between Staintondale and Ravenscar.
(Martin Bairstow)

The first Pinchinthorpe Station (1854 – 1877) still in use as a private residence. This is the outside. The other side of the building fronted onto the platforms. (Alan Young)

Nautical Interlude On a very wet 13 July 2007, the "Balmoral" made a rare excursion from Scarborough to Hartlepool, calling at Whitby where it tied up at the Endeavour Quay, near to the station. It is seen leaving Whitby, preceded by the pilot launch. *(John Holroyd)*

For many years it had been possible to sail from Scarborough to Whitby, once or twice a week in summer, aboard the "Coronia". In July 2007, the "Coronia" returned from a major refit, to be told by the Maritime & Coastguard Agency that "due to new European regulations", it could no longer sail more than 15 nautical miles from its port of *departure*. Whitby is 17. It was quickly discovered that European regulations have nothing to do with it. They say that a ship of this class may not sail more than 15 miles from a port of *refuge*. The "Coronia" and its fleet mate "Regal Lady" are now confined to non-landing cruises from Scarborough because the MCA declines to interpret or implement European regulations correctly. Regal Lady at Scarborough in September 2000. *(Martin Bairstow)*

The same fate has befallen the weekly Scarborough trip aboard the Bridlington based "Yorkshire Belle". The vessel, which once provided winter cover for the Hull – New Holland ferry, arrives at Scarborough on 13 July 2007, passing the "Balmoral" at the Lighthouse Pier. *(Martin Bairstow)*

Appendices

The Whitby & Pickering Railway

Opened		miles	Stations	opened	closed
Whitby – Grosmont	15. 5.1835	0	Whitby Town	15. 5.1835	–
Grosmont – Pickering	26. 5.1836	1 ½	Ruswarp	15. 5.1835	–
Pickering – Malton	7. 7.1845	3	Sleights	15. 5.1835	–
		6 ¼	Grosmont	15. 5.1835	–
Closed to passengers		–	Beck Hole	26. 5.1836	21. 9.1914
Grosmont – Beck Hole	21. 9.1914	9 ½	Goathland	26. 5.1836	6. 3.1965
Grosmont – Malton	6. 3.1965	15	Newtondale	13. 4.1981	
		18	Levisham	26. 5.1836	6. 3.1965
Closed to all traffic		24	Pickering	26. 5.1836	6. 3.1965
Grosmont – Beck Hole	1951	27 ½	Marishes Road	7. 7.1845	6. 3.1965
Grosmont – Pickering	6. 3.1965	30 ½	Rillington	7. 7.1845	20. 9.1930
Pickering – Rillington	1. 7.1966	35	Malton	7. 7.1845	–
Reopened					
Grosmont – Pickering	22. 4.1973				

The new route between Deviation Junction (Grosmont) and Goathland Summit opened on 1.7.1865 and the old route was abandoned south of Beck Hole. A summer only passenger service was restored between Grosmont and Beck Hole in 1908. Goathland Station was resited when the deviation opened in 1865. Goathland, Levisham and Pickering stations reopened on 22.4.1973 though Pickering was on a temporary site until 24.5.1975.

Scarborough – Whitby – Saltburn

Opened			miles	Stations	opened	closed
			0	Scarborough Central	7. 7.1845	–
Loftus – Skinningrove (goods)	27. 5.1867		2 ¾	Scalby	16. 7.1885	28. 2.1953
Skinningrove – Brotton (goods)	21. 4.1865		5	Cloughton	16. 7.1885	6. 3.1965
Brotton – Saltburn (goods)	1. 7.1872		7	Hayburn Wyke	16. 7.1885	6. 3.1965
Loftus – Saltburn (passenger)	1. 4.1875		8	Stainton Dale	16. 7.1885	6. 3.1965
Whitby Town – Loftus	3.12.1883		10 ¼	Ravenscar	16. 7.1885	6. 3.1965
Scarborough – Prospect Hill Jn	16. 7.1885		13 ½	Fyling Hall	16. 7.1885	6. 3.1965
Closed to passengers			15 ¼	Robin Hood's Bay	16. 7.1885	6. 3.1965
Brotton – Saltburn	6. 9.1957		18 ½	Hawsker	16. 7.1885	6. 3.1965
Whitby West Cliff – Loftus	3. 5.1958		–	Whitby Town	15. 5.1835	–
Loftus – Brotton	30. 4.1960		21 ¾	Whitby West Cliff	3.12.1883	10. 6.1961
Prospect Hill Jn – West Cliff	10. 6.1961		23 ¾	Sandsend	3.12.1883	3. 5.1958
Scarborough – Whitby Town	6. 3.1965		26 ¾	Kettleness	3.12.1883	3. 5.1958
Closed to all traffic			30	Hinderwell	3.12.1883	3. 5.1958
Whitby West Cliff – Loftus	3. 5.1958		31 ¾	Staithes	3.12.1883	3. 5.1958
Prospect Hill Jn – West Cliff	10. 6.1961		35 ¼	Grinkle	3.12.1883	10. 9.1939
Loftus – Skinningrove	10. 8.1963		36 ½	Loftus	1. 4.1875	30. 4.1960
Gallows Close – Whitby Town	6. 3.1965		37 ½	Skinningrove	1. 4.1875	28. 6.1952
Falsgrave Jn – Gallows Close	1981		41 ¼	Brotton	1. 4.1875	30. 4.1960
Reopened			42 ¾	North Skelton	1902	8. 9.1951
Skinningrove – Boulby	1. 4.1974		45 ½	Saltburn	17. 8.1861	–

Middlesbrough – Guisborough – Esk Valley – Whitby

Opened				miles	Stations	opened	closed
Grosmont – Whitby	15. 5.1835			0	Middlesbrough	27.12.1830	–
Middlesbrough – Guisborough (goods)	11.11.1853			3	Ormesby (Marton)	25. 2.1854	–
Middlesbrough – Guisborough (passenger)	25. 2.1854			4	Gypsy Lane	3. 5.1976	–
Picton – Stokesley	3. 3.1857			4 ½	Nunthorpe	25. 2.1854	–
Stokesley – Ingleby (goods)	1. 2.1858		7 ½		Pinchinthorpe	25. 2.1854	27.10.1951
Ingleby – Kildale (goods)	6. 4.1858		8 ¾		Hutton Gate	1. 1.1904	29. 2.1964
Battersby – West Rosedale (goods)	27. 3.1861		10		Guisborough	25. 2.1854	29. 2.1964
Kildale – Castleton (goods)	1. 4.1861		14		Boosbeck	1.11.1878	30. 4.1960
Stokesley – Castleton (passenger)	1. 4.1861		16 ¾		Brotton	1. 4.1875	30. 4.1960
Guisborough – Boosbeck (goods)	1862		18 ½		Skinningrove	1. 4.1875	28. 6.1952
Boosbeck – Brotton (goods)	23. 2.1865		19 ½		Loftus	1. 4.1875	30. 4.1960
Brotton – Skinningrove (goods)	Apr 1865		8 ¼		Great Ayton	1. 4.1868	–
Blakey Jn – East Rosedale (goods)	18. 8.1865		0		Picton	2. 6.1852	2. 1.1960
Castleton – Grosmont	2.10.1865		2		Trenholme Bar	3. 3.1857	12. 6.1954
Skinningrove – Loftus (goods)	27. 5.1867		4 ¼		Potto	3. 3.1857	12. 6.1954
Brotton – Loftus (passenger)	1. 4.1875		5 ¼		Sexhow	3. 3.1857	12. 6.1954
Guisborough – Brotton (passenger)	1.11.1878		8 ½		Stokesley	3. 3.1857	12. 6.1954
Closed to passengers			11 ½		Ingleby	1. 4.1861	12. 6.1954
Picton – Battersby	12. 6.1954	11	12		Battersby	1. 4.1861	–
Guisborough – Loftus	30. 4.1960		12 ¾		Kildale	1. 4.1861	–
Nunthorpe – Guisborough	29. 2.1964		16 ¾		Commondale	1. 4.1861	–
			18 ½		Castleton Moor	1. 4.1861	–
Closed to all traffic			19 ¾		Danby	2.10.1865	–
Battersby – West and East Rosedale	24. 1.1929		23 ½		Lealholm	2.10.1865	–
Picton – Stokesley	29.11.1958		25 ½		Glaisdale	2.10.1865	–
Guisborough – Boosbeck	30. 4.1960		27 ¼		Egton	2.10.1865	–
Skinningrove – Loftus	10. 8.1963		28 ¾		Grosmont	15. 5.1835	–
Boosbeck – Brotton	12. 9.1964		32		Sleights	15. 5.1835	–
Stokesley – Battersby	31. 7.1965		33 ½		Ruswarp	15. 5.1835	–
			35		Whitby Town	15. 5.1835	–

The Ryedale Lines

		miles	Stations	opened	closed
Opened		0	Pilmoor	17. 6.1847	3. 5.1958
Pilmoor – Malton	19. 5.1853	4	Husthwaite Gate	19. 5.1853	31. 1.1953
Bishophouse Jn – Sunbeck Jn	9.10.1871	5½	Coxwold	19. 5.1853	31. 1.1953
Gilling – Hemsley	9.10.1871	7¾	Ampleforth	19. 5.1853	3. 6.1950
Helmsley – Kirbymoorside	1. 1.1874	10½	Gilling	19. 5.1853	31. 1.1953
Kirbymoorside – Pickering	1. 4.1875	14	Hovingham Spa	19. 5.1853	30.12.1930
		16	Slingsby	19. 5.1853	30.12.1930
Closed to passengers		17½	Barton-le-Street	19. 5.1853	30.12.1930
Gilling – Malton	30.12.1930	19¼	Amotherby	19. 5.1853	30.12.1930
Raskelf – Pickering	31. 1.1953	23½	Malton	7. 7.1845	–
		13½	Nunnington	9.10.1871	31. 1.1953
Closed to all traffic		14¾	Helmsley	9.10.1871	31. 1.1953
Kirbymoorside – Pickering	31. 1.1953	19¾	Nawton	1. 1.1874	31. 1.1953
Bishophouse Jn – Sunbeck Jn	Sep 1955	22½	Kirbymoorside	1. 1.1874	31. 1.1953
Pilmoor – Husthwaite Gate	8. 9.1962	25½	Sinnington	1. 4.1875	31. 1.1953
Husthwaite Gate – Amotherby	7. 8.1964	29½	Pickering	7. 7.1845	6. 3.1965
Gilling – Kirbymoorside	7. 8.1964				
Amotherby – Malton	16.10.1964				

The Forge Valley Line

		miles	Stations	opened	closed
Opened		0	Pickering	7. 7.1845	6. 3.1965
Pickering – Seamer	1. 5.1882	3	Thornton Dale	1. 5.1882	3. 6.1950
		5¾	Ebberston	1. 5.1882	3. 6.1950
Closed to passengers		8¼	Snainton	1. 5.1882	3. 6.1950
Pickering – Seamer	3. 6.1950	10	Sawdon	1. 5.1882	3. 6.1950
Closed to all traffic		11¾	Wykeham	1. 5.1882	3. 6.1950
Thornton Dale – Seamer	3. 6.1950	13¼	Forge Valley	1. 5.1882	3. 6.1950
Pickering – Thornton Dale	25. 1.1963	16¾	Seamer	7. 7.1845	–

Class B16 No 61461 accelerates away from Scarborough Road Junction and crosses the main line with a Saturday Scarborough to Glasgow train in July 1961.
(D Butterfield)

Conclusion

Once a track alignment has been lost, it can be a prohibitively lengthy and expensive process to regain it. Some of the Beeching closures, for example, have resulted in the loss of routes that would be extremely valuable to today's railway. – Department for Transport (2006)

It would be difficult to argue with that, except to advance the view that Rillington Junction to Pickering was one such route.

The town of Whitby today is busy. A direct rail service from York would be well used, far more so on a year round basis than it was pre 1965. Whitby retains a rail link, but its connection to the main body of the network is so tenuous that it caters virtually for local traffic only.

Whitby Station, the bit that's not buried under a supermarket, is now handling more business than at any time since 1965, thanks to the North Yorkshire Moors Railway. Whilst this is a tremendous achievement, it does nothing to restore Whitby's main line connection.

If the Malton to Grosmont line had never been closed, there would be no NYMR, no steam on the Moors, no Levisham or Newtondale Halt, just a regular service of DMUs heading semi fast to Whitby. But did the Founders of the NYMR not come together in 1967 to consider preserving a part of *either* the Whitby & Pickering or the Scarborough & Whitby lines? If the main line had survived for through traffic, we might now be watching steam slogging up from Whitby to Prospect Hill, over Larpool Viaduct and on to Robin Hoods Bay and Ravenscar.

The NYMR Whitby "extension" seems to have been a success. Getting more out of the Middlesbrough line is difficult. Except perhaps in its northern extreme where there is significant population and where there is line capacity for a more intensive service, which has already begun to emerge. I suggested earlier in the book that there might also be scope for a commuter service between Saltburn and Loftus. That would use a section of line, which lay not derelict but abandoned between 1963 and 1974.

The ultimate goal would be to reinstate the 6½ miles between Rillington and Pickering.